6G Visions for a Sustainable and People-centric Future
From Communications to Services, the CONASENSE Perspective

RIVER PUBLISHERS SERIES IN COMMUNICATIONS AND NETWORKING

Series Editors:

ABBAS JAMALIPOUR
The University of Sydney
Australia

MARINA RUGGIERI
University of Rome Tor Vergata
Italy

The "River Publishers Series in Communications and Networking" is a series of comprehensive academic and professional books which focus on communication and network systems. Topics range from the theory and use of systems involving all terminals, computers, and information processors to wired and wireless networks and network layouts, protocols, architectures, and implementations. Also covered are developments stemming from new market demands in systems, products, and technologies such as personal communications services, multimedia systems, enterprise networks, and optical communications.

The series includes research monographs, edited volumes, handbooks and textbooks, providing professionals, researchers, educators, and advanced students in the field with an invaluable insight into the latest research and developments.

Topics included in this series include:-

- Communication theory
- Multimedia systems
- Network architecture
- Optical communications
- Personal communication services
- Telecoms networks
- Wi-Fi network protocols

For a list of other books in this series, visit www.riverpublishers.com

6G Visions for a Sustainable and People-centric Future

From Communications to Services, the CONASENSE Perspective

Editors

Ramjee Prasad

CTIF, Aarhus University, Denmark

Rute C. Sofia

fortiss GmbH, Germany

NEW YORK AND LONDON

Published 2024 by River Publishers
River Publishers
Alsbjergvej 10, 9260 Gistrup, Denmark
www.riverpublishers.com

Distributed exclusively by Routledge
605 Third Avenue, New York, NY 10017, USA
4 Park Square, Milton Park, Abingdon, Oxon OX14 4RN

6G Visions for a Sustainable and People-centric Future / by Ramjee Prasad,
Rute C. Sofia.

Routledge is an imprint of the Taylor & Francis Group, an informa
business

ISBN 978-87-7022-751-3 (hardback)
ISBN 978-87-7004-016-7 (paperback)
ISBN 978-10-0096-569-8 (online)
ISBN 978-10-0344-939-3 (master ebook)

While every effort is made to provide dependable information, the
publisher, authors, and editors cannot be held responsible for any errors
or omissions.

Contents

Preface

6G is currently under the definition, being often addressed from a plain telecommunications perspective, as an evolutionary paradigm that represents an extension of 5G. Having a horizon 2030, 6G initiatives are being deployed across the globe, to further ignite the development of 6G services. In its philosophy core, 6G embodies the "human in the loop" principle. The research effort being developed towards 6G requires an interdisciplinary approach that ignites discussion across different key technological sectors, ranging from communications to services and business cases.

The contributions of this book to research in the field concern an evolutionary and interdisciplinary design of 6G as a paradigm that can be addressed by working together 4 different computational areas: communications; satellites and navigation; sensing; services.

The book derives from initial brainstorming that has been developed during the 11th CONASENSE symposium[1] held in October 2021 in fortiss, Munich, Germany, being jointly hosted by CTIF, Aarhus University, Denmark, and fortiss, Germany. Several international experts contribute to an overview of 6G key challenges; new networking trends, and challenges to be overcome; advanced 6G services.

The book starts with a perspective on 6G challenges and use-cases beyond the 2030 horizon, to then continue to address the role of non-terrestrial networks and cognitive, service-centric satellite networks in future 6G services. Still, with a focus on 6G adaptive networking, the book continues with a debate on the need to integrate social awareness based on an interdisciplinary approach in network operations. Then, specific examples of advanced services (quantum imaging and holography; localization of IoT Remote Things) are discussed.

---

[1] http://www.conasense.org/CONASENSE_International_Symposium_2021.php

The book is, therefore, envisioned to assist in developing critical thinking to back up novel networking, applications, and services towards 6G.

Editors:

Rute C. Sofia
fortiss GmbH, Germany

Ramjee Prasad
CTIF, Aarhus University, Denmark

Acknowledgement

Acknowledgement is due to the international experts in 6G that attended and participated in the 11th CONASENSE workshop, held on October 4th and 5th 2021 in fortiss, Munich, Germany, and in hybrid mode.

The opinions expressed in the book are those of the editors, authors, and contributors and do not necessarily represent those of any organizations, employers, or companies.

List of Figures

List of Tables

List of Contributors

Chen, Kwan-Cheng, *University of South Florida, USA*

Cianca, Ernestina, *University of Rome Tor Vergata, Italy*

de Cola, Tomaso, *DLR, Germany*

de Sanctis, Mauro, *University of Rome Tor Vergata, Italy*

McElroy, Joseph, *University of South Florida, USA*

Mendes, Paulo M., *Airbus, Germany*

Prasad, Ramjee, *CTIF, Aarhus University, Denmark*

Rossi, Tommaso, *University of Rome Tor Vergata, Italy*

Rufino Henrique, Paulo Sergio, *CTIF, Aarhus University, Denmark*

Sofia, Rute C., *fortiss, GmbH*

List of Abbreviations

3GPP	3rd generation partnership project
5G NR	5G new radio
5G-IA	5G infrastructure association
AAA	Authentication, authorization, accounting
AI	Artificial intelligence
AP	Access Point
AR	Augmented reality
B5G	Beyond 5G
BNet	Bayesian network
CCN	Content centric networking
CGC	CTIF global capsule
CMM	Community mobility modeling
CMM	Community mobility model
CN	5G Core network
CU-DU	5G centralized unit-distributed unit
D2D	Device to device
DLT	Distributed ledger technology
DSL	Domain specific language
DTN	Delay/disruption tolerant networking
DWDM	Dense wavelength division multiplexing
EDRS	European data relay service
eMBB	Enhanced mobile broadband
EO	Earth observation
ETSI	European telecommunications standards institute
FIB	Forwarding information database
FSO	Free-space optics
GEO	Geosynchronous equatorial orbit
gNB	G Node B, 5G base station
HAPS	High-altitude platform systems
HyDRON	High throughput optical networks
IAB	Integrated-access and backhaul

ICN	Information-centric networking
IoT	Internet of things
IRIS	Internet routing in space
ISL	Inter-satellite links
KPI	Key performance indicators
LEO	Low orbit earth observation
LEO	Low earth orbit
M2M	Machine to machine
MCS	Mobile crowd sensing
MEO	Medium earth orbit
ML	Machine learning
mMTC	Massive machine type communications
NDN	Named data networking
NFaaS	Named function as a service
NFN	Named function networking
NFV	Network function virtualization
NGSO	Non-geostationary orbit (NGSO)
NOMA	Non-orthogonal multiple access
NSH	Network service header
NTN	Non-terrestrial networks
OBP	On-board processing
ONAP	Open network automation platform
OSN	Online social network
PNN	Probabilistic neural networks
QKD	Quantum key distribution
QML	Quantum machine learning
QoE	Quality of experience
QoS	Quality of service
RAN	Radio access network
RDF	Resource description framework
RF	Radio frequency
RIS	Reconfigurable intelligent surfaces
RLLC	Ultra reliable low latency communication
ROADM	Reconfigurable optical add-drop multiplexer
RTT	Round trip time
SAT	Service action times
SDG	Sustainable development goals
SDN	Software defined networking
SFC	Service function chaining

SIMPS	Sociological interaction mobility for population simulation
SLA	Service level agreement
SLO	Service level objectives
SLS	Service level specification
TOSCA	Orchestration specification for cloud applications
UE	User equipment
VPP	Vector packet processing
VR	Virtual reality
Wi-Fi	Wireless fidelity

1

Introduction

Rute C. Sofia and Ramjee Prasad

Rute C. Sofia, fortiss research institute for software intensive services and systems, Germany,
Ramjee Prasad, CGC, Aarhus University, Denmark,
E-mail: sofia@fortiss.org; ramjee@btech.au.dk

The 6G paradigm is currently the focus of a large number of scientific domains, in an effort to reach the desired always-on, sustainable, and efficient human-centric services, that assist in the development of mankind. Sustainability, affordability, flexibility, and accessibility are among the main drivers toward 6G services. Of relevancy to 6G is the capability of the overall holistic systems to support connectivity across very diverse geographic regions, considering that a large share of the human population (over 3.5 billion) does not yet have Internet access.

For 6G to become a reality until 2030 and beyond, several efforts are being developed across the globe and across different scientific domains. Across Europe, several initiatives such as 5G-IA/5G-PPP,[1] one6G, ThinkNet6G,[2] and 6G-IA[3] are providing platforms for the debate of 6G, with focus on networking adaptations and focus on the *European Sustainable Development Goals (SDG)*. Across the USA, different initiatives are also rising, such as the Department of Defense Open6G[4] industry-academia cooperative research center focused on future open, programmable, and disaggregated 6G systems.

However, these initiatives are mostly focused on technological developments, based on key societal drivers such as sustainability and affordability.

---

[1] https://5g-ppp.eu/european-vision-for-the-6g-network-ecosystem/.

[2] https://www.bayern-innovativ.de/de/netzwerke-und-thinknet/uebersicht-digitalisierung/thinknet-6g.

[3] https://6g-ia.eu/.

[4] https://open6g.wiot.northeastern.edu/.

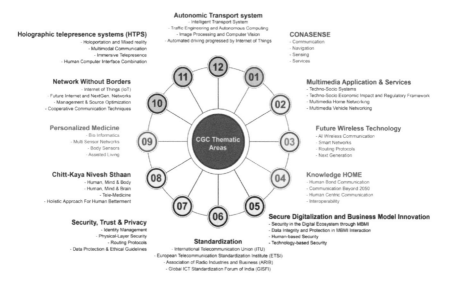

Figure 1.1   The CTIF 12 research branches.

For 6G to become a reality, it is relevant to address the societal development it may bring, along with the economical and technological advancements.

Initiatives that focus on the human-in-the-loop 6G approach are also rising, focusing on use cases that may benefit society, based on the holistic 6G approach.[5]

CONASENSE[6] falls into the category of 6G discussion and brainstorming platforms that aim at providing a holistic, human-centric perspective to 6G services and technologies. For that purpose, CONASENSE means "Communication, Navigation, Sensing, and Services" and is one of the 12 international research branches of the *Core Tele Infrastructure Global Capsule (CGC)* institute of Aarhus University, see Figure 1.1. CONASENSE has been started in 2012[7] and has been dedicated to the beyond 5G/6G discussion of services based on the four mentioned areas.

Since 2021, CONASENSE as a 6G debate and discussion platform is being developed jointly by CGC, Aarhus University, in cooperation with

---

[5]https://5g-ppp.eu/wp-content/uploads/2022/05/What-societal-values-will-6G-address-White-Paper-v1.0-final.pdf.

[6]http://www.conasense.org/.

[7]http://www.conasense.org/Talks/OpeningSession/Ramjee_Prasad_The%20CONASEN SE%20Vision.pdf.

fortiss, Munich. As an open platform, different activities, including brain-storming meetings with international experts, are being developed in the context of CONASENSE, focusing on the debate of 6G directions and challenges.

"Visions for a sustainable and people-centric future" provide the perspective of several 6G international experts toward new directions in networking, challenges to overcome, and making relevant 6G services a reality.

This book starts with an introduction to challenges and uses cases beyond the 6G horizon of 2030; it then provides a debate on new aspects related to holistic interdisciplinary networking aspects and ends with a debate on relevant 6G services.

This book is, therefore, envisioned to assist in developing critical thinking to back up 6G networking aspects, based on a people-centric, sustainable perspective.

1.1 Goals

This book provides the perspective of different experts in the context of the CONASENSE 6G vision, where next-generation services require an interdisciplinary and intertwined approach between communications, navigation and sensing, and service development. The core of this vision relies on reaching efficient, people-centric, and sustainable 6G services.

The main goals, from an audience perspective, are as follows:

- Globally, to become acquainted with the latest insights on 6G by key aspects and the challenges to overcome across communications, satellite networks, services, and sustainable business modeling.
- To better understand the challenges that are being addressed within the vast context of the 6G paradigm; how to assist its evolution; and the implications that may arise based on practical experience in operational fields.
- To acquire interdisciplinary knowledge, derived from the CONASENSE vision, on 6G services and challenges thereof.

1.2 Structure

This book is based on a modular format with eight distinct chapters.

Chapter 1 introduces the motivation and structure.

Chapter 2 (*Paulo Sergio Rufino Henrique, Ramjee Prasad*) provides an overview of challenges and use cases beyond 2030, based on the CONASENSE vision to 6G services.

Chapters 3–5 introduce new aspects related to holistic and interdisciplinary approaches for 6G networking aspects. Specifically,

Chapter 3 (*Tomaso de Cola*) debates on non-terrestrial networks (NTN) as a key enabler of the 6G-NTN networking concept, surveying the main concepts explored so far in the context of integrated and 5G networks, and develops further new concepts for the effective integration of NTN in the upcoming new generation of cellular networks, namely, 6G.

Chapter 4 (*Paulo Mendes*) debates on the required support of more flexible, scalable, and low-cost management of cognitive networks in the context of a 6G heterogeneous infrastructure integrating large-scale deployments of smart satellites.

Chapter 5 (*Rute C. Sofia*) introduces the need to integrate an interdisciplinary approach for context awareness derived from social sciences, in particular, social psychology, and computer science to support diverse 6G services, proposing initial steps to address this integration.

A debate on relevant 6G services is provided in Chapters 6 and 7. Specifically, **Chapter 6** (*Kwang-Chen Cheng*) introduces quantum imaging and holography, which is expected to be one of the most relevant services to be supported in 6G environments.

Chapter 7 (*Ernestina Cianca, Mauro de Sanctis, Thomas Rossi*) addresses localization challenges for the deployment of 6G Internet of Remote Things services, providing an overview of the current 5G directions and outlining challenges and research directions to take into consideration toward 6G.

Chapter 8 concludes this book and provides a perspective toward future developments in 6G.

2

CONASENSE, Challenges, and Use Cases Beyond 2030

Paulo Sergio Rufino Henrique[1] and Ramjee Prasad[2]

[1]Paulo Rufino, CGC, Aarhus University, Denmark
[2]CTIF, Aarhus University, Denmark, France
Email: rufino@spideo.tv

Abstract

The completed integration of communication, navigation, sensing, and services is the real motivation for the CONASENSE Networks (CNSS). With the advent of mobile broadband communications, all the first three areas of CONASENSE are becoming essential for digital services. This chapter looks into the importance of having such integrated areas operating in perfect harmony and optimized for any new and future services. To begin, an analysis of the current state of the art of 5G networks is presented, followed by the challenges of creating an intelligent CNSS. Afterward, an evaluation of how these CNSS principles can be employed in the future 6G networks is presented. From quantum computing and quantum machine learning to advanced artificial intelligence (AI) to be part of the 6G Cognitive Radio blueprint. Finally, some use cases are highlighted using CONASENSE architecture to address societal and environmental use cases beyond 2030, such as Society 5.0 and United Nations Sustainable Development Goals (SDGs).

Keywords: 6G, AI, CONASENSE, CNSS, Cognitive Radio, Quantum Computing, Quantum Machine Learning, SDGs, Society 5.0.

2.1 Introduction

The integration of communication, navigation, sensing, and services are the four key areas that combined generated the acronym of CONASENSE. Integrating these areas had been the motivation for the creation of this research area [1]. Nowadays, more and more applications and services depend on the synergy of CONASENSE. At the same time, it is expected that CONASENSE also improves the *quality of service (QoS)* and the user-perceived *quality of experience (QoE)* for current 5G use cases, and future 6G use cases. For instance, unmanned automated vehicles (UAVs)/automated guide vehicles/mobile robots-based services; *Internet of Things (IoT)* services; aeronautics services; e-health; Smart Cities; Green businesses [2]; and the Metaverse are just a few services to benefit from these innovations.

Thus, the advancement of CONASENSE's CNSS architecture directly impacts many vertical and horizontal research areas. The international, cross-interdisciplinary, and academic research center, known as *Core Tele Infrastructure Global Capsule (CGC)* [3], has also chosen CONASENSE as one of its priorities of investigation in its vertical thematic research areas. As illustrated in Figure 2.1, CONASENSE primarily aims to promote the full integration of communication, navigation, and sensing to offer 6G advanced services and beyond. Additionally, the picture has a white cloud surrounding the atom showing the integrated areas – this white cloud represents several probabilities that can propel or degrade services depending on this network.

However, why is deploying CONASENSE important? Improving the end-to-end services currently not in sync with the wireless communication technologies is vital. For example, sensing does not always have the best communication channel to deliver the future growth of IIoT. Having said that, 5G New Radio (NR) release 17 has embedded the *Ultra Reliable Low Latency Communication (URLLC)* features to deliver such improvement for IoT services and machine-to-machine communications. Additionally, in the same 5G NR entity exists the architecture for RAN Slicing, Positioning, and *Extended Reality (XR)* NR. As a continued evolution *Beyond 5G (B5G)*, the 6G KPIs vary between ten to a hundred times more critical than IMT-2020. In this case, a 6G evolution of the current 5G NR is also expected. For instance, in the positioning area, in which CONASENSE is mapped with navigation, it will require precision down to a centimeter for special critical services, like the evolution of services for Industry 4.0, drones, and autonomous vehicles.

On the other hand, the 6G evolution of the 5G *enhanced Mobile Broadband (eMBB)* is also expected. When a close caption on the architecture of

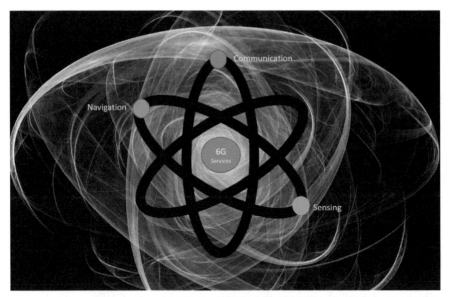

Figure 2.1 CONASENSE integration for 6G services.

5G eMBB is made, it is clear that the current MIMO improvements will evolve to MASSIVE-MIMO solutions, and the QoE will also be part of the 6G Radio, especially considering the coverage. For this part, the CNSS node is responsible for it, it is the communication. As further developed in this chapter, the dream of a ubiquitous network will also depend on a 6G cognitive radio orchestration of diverse types of heterogeneous networks down to the physical layer, such as a combined combination. The CNSS communication node will also require attention due to the contribution of tackling the digital divide, especially since almost 50% of the world population does not have access to the Internet and is not participating in the mobile economy. Humanity has learned during the current pandemic situation caused by the spread of COVID-19 that the most vulnerable people were the ones that lived at the margin of the mobile economy. As the UN has announced that by December 2022, the world population will reach the historical number of eight billion inhabitants [4], and digital inclusion is a crucial topic of the SDGs that needs to be overseen.

Lastly, despite the technologies in use to deploy 6G and attend to its services and roadmap [5], CNSS will benefit from Cloud services architectures and quantum technologies to provide excellent computing power and reverse computing. Quantum technologies will be responsible for offering a robust security service addition to the DLT and driving the optimization of *Probabilistic Neural Networks (PNNs)* based on quantum machine learning *(QML)* [6].

2.2 CONASENSE Challenges, Present, and Future

The complete integration of CNSS is a challenge due to the nature of each instance of its architecture. Communication, navigation, and sensing (3C-CNSS) represent the instances placed at the heart of CONASENSE as nodes to achieve what is expected in the service part. As can be seen from Figure 2.2, each CNSS node has a different set of KPIs to measure QoS and QoE for services due to its independent nature. All of this happens due to the intrinsic characteristics of the nodes and their correlation with the network environment. As a result, the CNSS network has many variables, generating high uncertainty in predicting how all nodes will interact.

Looking at CNSS nodes, one can infer to evaluate some probabilities of failures or degraded services that might occur in each CNSS node. For this, a simple inference is applied and shown in Table 2.1 and its SMART methodology [7]. The SMART methodology helps present the KPIs, which also were derived from known network cases, 5G KPIs, and the 6G as explained in Table 2.1.

Thus, artificial intelligence (AI) is needed to have such a great number of variables to control the best QoS and QoE for 6G Services. In this sense,

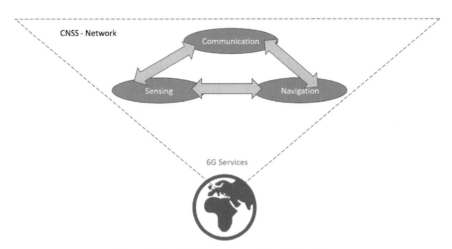

Figure 2.2   CNSS concept and the 6G services.

Table 2.1 CNSS KPIs vs. causes of failures and degradations.

3C-CNSS node	Medium/topology	Failure/degradation (causes) SMART KPIs
Communication	Wireless, Fixed, Satellites, OWC	Latency, packet loss, jitter, synchronization between communication components, connection density, bandwidth, mobility, mobility interruption time, coverage area
Navigation	Wireless, Fixed, Satellites, OWC	Mobility, mobility interruption time, location accuracy, availability, Known geographical, Unknown geographical, speed, coverage area
Sensing	WAN, MAN, LAN, PAN	Transmission range, Transmission accuracy, downlink, uplink, location accuracy, loss rate, vulnerability

machine learning (ML) is the proposed AI solution to handle the probability distribution of each node of CNSS. As considered previously, an approach with PNN can be applied to find the optimal results for a given CNSS and its random variables. Therefore, the *Bayesian network (BNet)* [8] is the specific PNN to be studied in this chapter to realize CONASENSE for 6G. BNets, also known as *belief nets*, permit to feed machine learning algorithms to optimize the best results for uncertain models for the CNSS. With this, a BNet applied for the CONASENSE will be able to predict, forecast accurately, and offer anomaly recognition. Figure 2.3 shows the CONASENSE BNet concept based on the ML Inference concept.

As there are four nodes in total in the CNSS, considering services, one of the last activities will be to create a BNet to factorize the number of

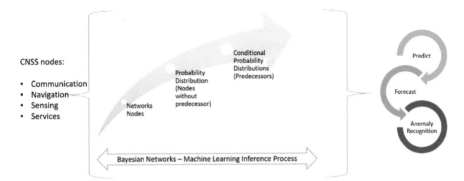

Figure 2.3 CONASENSE Bayesian networks.

nodes to find out the possible number of Bayesian networks that need to construct. Through factorization, the number of possible BNets will be 24. Then the acyclic graph model for CNSS can be created for these 24 variables, and the ML can be fed together with the KPIs mentioned in Table 2.1. In summary, utilizing BNets seems promising to offer an optimized solution for the vast random variables to be considered in the CNSS nodes. However, let us analyze how this model would fit into the 6G services.

2.3 CONASENSE Orchestrated for 6G Services

6G is the next generation of mobile broadband networks. Its roadmap is being built to overcome many obstacles and use cases not possible to be covered in the 5G releases. However, societal values are the main drivers for the 6G ecosystem for the first time. Consequently, SDGs and Society 5.0 are at the center of its development. The current and next decades are in need of an intelligent network that can meet all these societal and environmental requirements. As present in the heart of Society 5.0, the fusion of the physical and the cyber world will be a gain to offer an extra quality of life to humanity. Also, the growth of the cyberworld, which has been renamed *Metaverse*, is in great acceleration. The main limitation of its services is network infrastructure. The Metaverse market is expected to grow by 5 trillion US dollars by 2030 [9]. Therefore, 6G must be able to match this expectation by offering an omnipresent network and, at the same time, intelligent to deal with different requirements and SLAs.

Think about the 6G services with the combined societal drivers; a few areas of CONASENS impact can be envisaged and presented here. Some areas of services that CONASENSE can help accelerate their integration into the 6G ecosystem are as follows:

- Holographic type communication
- Smart cities and E-recycle waste
- Automotive (autonomous vehicles)
- E-education (distance learning)
- E-health and wellness
- Agriculture
- Aerospace
- Geo positioning systems
- Satellites communications
- Space industries

- IIoT
- Climate change/climate surveillance
- Green business
- Smart meters and energy
- Critical services

In summary, the 6G services are vast, and the number of devices connected to the 6G network by 2030 will be immense, following the recent forecasts. For that reason, the data traffic will grow exponentially, pushing the computer power for processing data streaming at the end of the network to extremes. Thus, considering this fact, supercomputer power will be required to process data at the edge and for machine learning purposes, which also considers security measures.

In order to be ready for such a Big Data challenge and the massive number of devices connectivity by 2030, quantum technologies are considered to tackle these problems. As ML is being deployed in many areas, training ML algorithms is becoming a laborious task. Therefore, quantum computers forged with ML can offer an advantage in solving this challenge. Hence, to emulate the Bayesian network for CONASENSE and get the best optimal result, *QML* is a tool to explore.

The critical characteristic of *QML* applied for CONASENSE is that the speed to factorize the number of random variables on the CNSS nodes will be much faster than the one carried out on classical computation. All of this is thanks to the quantum computing power offered to deal with reverse computing based on the physical phenomenon of quantum entanglement, superposition, and interference. This is the proposed architecture to be explored in the CONASENSE research area, which is to build a QML to optimize the results of a Bayesian network for the CNSS part.

2.4 Conclusions

Accelerating the integration of all CONASENSE [10] areas is a big challenge for the next ten years. But it is not impossible, especially if it is considered to deploy machine learning to estimate optimal results when part of the CNSS notes has been degraded or failed. Once this process has been mastered, it can contribute to the 6G intelligent network for offering the desired excellent user experience in all future services. As a mechanism to support such integration, there are Bayesian networks combined with the Machine Learning process to forecast and identify anomalies in the causal effects of the CNSS nodes based on their KPIs. Finally, testing this theory with quantum computers is a differential as such technology can offer the excellent computer power required to perform such ML algorithms. However, the current drawbacks are related to the available quantum computer or simulator in classical computers that have a physical limitation of quantum bits (Qbits) to perform such tasks. However, the next step of the author's investigation in this topic is to partially simulate some of the CNSS KPIs in a quantum computer environment with Bayesian functions.

Acknowledgements

The authors thank Supreme Energy and their family for such support in the long hours of studies and laborious work.

References

[1] "Communications- navigation-sensing-services," Communications-Navigation-Sensing-Services. [Online]. Available:http://conasense.org/ .[Accessed:1-Jul-2022].

[2] P. Lindgren, "6G Technologies – How Can It Help Future Green Business Model Innovation," Journal of ICT Standardization. [Online]. Available: https://journals.riverpublishers.com/index.php/JICTS/article /view/8981.[Accessed:15-Jul-2022].

[3] CTIF Global Capsule. [Online]. Available: https://ctifglobalcapsule.or g/about/our-team/.[Accessed:20-Jul-2022].

[4] United Nations, "The global population will soon reach 8 billion-then what?," United Nations, 11-Jul-2022. [Online]. Available: https://www. un.org/en/un-chronicle/global-population-will-soon-reach-8-billion-t hen-what.[Accessed:13-Jul-2022].

[5] P. S. Rufino Henrique and R. Prasad, "6G The Road to the Future Wireless Technologies 2030," River Publishers: Professional Books, 31-Mar-2021. [Online]. Available: https://www.riverpublishers.com/book _details.php?book_id=920.[Accessed:13-Jul-2022].

[6] P. S. Rufino Henrique and R. Prasad, "The Road for 6G Multimedia Applications," 2020 23rd International Symposium on Wireless Personal Multimedia Communications (WPMC), 2020, pp. 1-6, doi: 10.1109/WPMC50192.2020.9309478.

[7] C. Fernández-Prades, "16 design forces for software-defined GNSS receivers," GNSS, 17-Jul-2022. [Online]. Available: https://gnss-sdr.org/design-forces/#fn:Doran81.[Accessed:19-Jul-2022].

[8] "Bayesian networks," BayesFusion. [Online]. Available: https://www.bayesfusion.com/bayesian-networks/?gclid=CjwKCAjwnZaVBhA6EiwAVVyv9HcychmK2FoNv1nirg5XsGFm-hAnzz36nDN00m_xaJQ0iR_0Fa0dHxoCoVEQAvD_BwE.[Accessed:14-Jul-2022].

[9] A. Pennington, "The metaverse will make $5 trillion by 2030. that sounds awesome and... wait, what are we talking about?," NAB Amplify, 14-Jul-2022. [Online]. Available: https://amplify.nabshow.com/articles/ic-the-metaverse-will-mean-5-trillion-up-by-2030/?utm_source=sfmc&utm_medium=email&utm_campaign=22AMP-Newsletter%2BMON%2B20220718&utm_term=https%3A%2F%2Famplify.nabshow.com%2Farticles%2Fic-the-metaverse-will-mean-5-trillion-up-by-2030%2F&utm_id=55066&sfmc_id=7381502.[Accessed:19-Jul-2022].

[10] P. Ligthart and R. Prasad, "Communications, navigation, sensing and services (CONASENSE)," River Publishers: Professional Books, 31-Mar-2013. [Online]. Available: https://www.riverpublishers.com/book_details.php?book_id=166.[Accessed:21-Jul-2022].

3

Non-terrestrial Networks as a Key Enabler for 5G Evolution Toward 6G

Tomaso de Cola

Tomaso de Cola, DLR, Germany,
Email: tomaso.decola@dlr.de

Abstract

Non-terrestrial networks (NTN) have proved to be pivotal components for the evolution of telecommunication networks since their conception in 2018 within 3GPP. Since then, further initiatives and projects have been ignited toward the convergence of NTN and 5G across different funding programs and frameworks within Europe, the United States, and Asia. This multilateral effort towards the inclusion of NTN into the definition of 5G-supported scenarios has hence helped in recognizing the value offered by NTN with respect to several application scenarios, usually embraced under the umbrella of "connecting the unconnected". Furthermore, the evidence brought by the benefits of deploying integrated NTN-5G networks has increased the awareness that the availability of NTN technologies will certainly represent a plus also in the design of 6G networks, in that terrestrial fixed and wireless infrastructures alone cannot cope with the "digital divide." As such NTN emerge as key component to achieve the so-called concept of 6G-NTN networks, building on new air interface, deep network programmability configuration, and data-driven design to fully exploit the power of AI schemes. The overall convergence of NTN and the rest of the 6G ecosystem has, however, to face important technical challenges given the nature of the NTN components, hence calling for new protocol concepts eventually resulting in a novel architectural design. To this end, this chapter surveys the main concepts explored so far in the context of integrated and 5G networks and develops

15

further new concepts for the effective integration of NTN in the upcoming new generation of cellular networks, namely 6G.

Keywords: Non-terrestrial Networks (NTN), SatCom, 6G, Network Architecture, Satellite Constellations, Edge Computing, NG-RAN.

3.1 Introduction

The increasing appeal of satellite communications observed in the last 5 years has been mostly determined by the renewed interest toward satellite constellations on the one hand and the emergence of the NTN concept within the 5G standardization process carried out within 3GPP [1]. As to the former, the *comeback* of satellite constellations has been characterized by the plan for systems composed of several hundreds or even thousands of satellites, hence composing the so-called satellite mega-constellations. The return of satellite constellation in the overall SatCom business is being also supported by more mature use cases and business plans in comparison to the first wave experienced at the end of years 1990s, which eventually resulted in just very few successful initiatives and in many failed plans. As to the latter, the conception of non-terrestrial networks within the 3GPP standardization process marks an important paradigm shift because satellite systems were never successfully integrated with the standardization process of cellular communication generation (except for the case of S-UMTS, which was, however, only a niche application) and on the contrary developed their markets and related use cases in isolation from the rest of the telecommunication ecosystem.

Despite these two important aspects, the integration of satellite systems (or NTN in a broad sense) into existing terrestrial infrastructures [2] is not coming at cost zero, because of the formidable technical challenges that must be tackled in order to come up with a unified system design. The vision of such a converged ecosystem building on heterogeneous networks (e.g., wireless terrestrial, fiber optics, and satellite) though starting already during the second phase of 5G standardization (i.e., during the specification work carried out in Rel. 17 until mid-2022) is far from being materialized in the short term period, given the usual transition phase necessary to finalize all experimental deployments and the let the market accept satellite-based systems integrated into 5G terrestrial counterparts. On the contrary, it is more meaningful to consider this phase as preparatory for the actual inclusion of NTN into the overall 6G-landscape [3], whose integration will happen through a more mature adoption of NTN-based solutions that will be validated in the course of the 5G-evolution path [4].

In more detail, the integration of non-terrestrial networks within the overall 5G/6G context requires important technical adaptation/extension in the satellite part, in both ground and space segments [5][6]. These are mostly related to the overall service-oriented and modular architecture applied in 5G terrestrial system, building on a functional separation across multiple components of the end-to-end communication system [7], whose implementation is importantly enabled by network function virtualization and by the overall network softwarization models. In this sense, particularly relevant for the integration of NTN into 6G systems is the extension of the network orchestration concepts already largely available for terrestrial systems [8], network slicing, end-to-end routing, edge computing, and resource allocation, just to name some of the key technical challenges.

This chapter surveys the main directions taken by NTN industry and academia to fill the technology gap with terrestrial system and effectively achieve integration in the overall 6G network ecosystem. In particular, the aforementioned technical areas will be analyzed with respect to the current literature, ongoing standardization efforts, as well as future directions toward the year 2030. Accordingly, the remainder of this chapter is structured as follows. Section 3.2 addresses the main use cases and related architectures envisioned in the context of 3GPP standardization [9]. A deeper analysis of the selected technical challenges is then given in Section 3.3. Future developments and new areas of research are then outlined in Section 3.4. Finally, the main conclusions from this survey are drawn in Section 3.5.

3.2 Integration of NTN and 5G/6G Systems

3.2.1 Relevant scenarios

Integration of NTN into nearly-happening 5G [10]-[12] and future 6G systems is envisioned as key enabler for a number of use cases, which have been classified into three main categories [1] in the course of the 3GPP 5G standardization, that is, (i) service continuity, (ii) service ubiquity, and (iii) service scalability.

The first one (i) deals mostly with the case of mobile nodes that along their path may not be able to get proper data connectivity offered by means of 5G terrestrial infrastructure only and on the contrary the availability of satellite systems may represent the means to guarantee service continuity. As such, the case of network switching or even the opportunity of exploiting multi-path communication paradigms is regarded as particularly attractive to this end.

The second scenario (ii) can be ultimately casted to the well-known set of un(der)served areas, where terrestrial connectivity is poor in terms of capacity offered to users or even completely absent. It is straightforward to see that these use cases correspond to remote areas where data connectivity can be only offered by satellites, since the morphological characteristics of that territory make cabling either not physically viable or in any case economically prohibitive because of the high deployment costs. Likewise, other scenarios where terrestrial connectivity is not an option are those related to maritime or aeronautical communications where only satellite is the means to guarantee data connectivity. Last but not the least, it is worth mentioning that data connectivity is not just a need of communities to provide population in villages with Internet access but has to do with the evolution of industry sector, so that agriculture precision is certainly benefitting from satellite connections for a more effective control and management of the production. It is also important to notice that all these scenarios address service ubiquity over a long-time frame, although also use-cases where the exploitation of satellite links happens for a shorter period of time are of key value. This is certainly the case of public safety or disaster management situations, during which natural or man-made hazards may cause temporary disruption of the terrestrial infrastructure. In such a case, the availability of a satellite link backup is necessary to guarantee data connectivity.

The last category, "service scalability" (iii), relates mostly to the possible exploitation of satellite systems for those services which require distribution on a large area simultaneously, whereby the intrinsic multicast/broadcast capability of satellites combined with the large coverage areas make their use particularly appealing. Moreover, this category also includes the case of simultaneous availability of terrestrial and satellite infrastructures, which in such a case may offer the possibility to offload the traffic from the terrestrial to the satellite counterpart, especially when a large bulk of non-real-time traffic can be better served by a satellite infrastructure without incurring in the risk of congesting terrestrial links, hence possibly affecting the timely distribution of real-time data flows.

Based on the aforementioned three use-case categories, more concrete exemplary scenarios can be identified, as shortly outlined below:

• Roaming between terrestrial and satellite networks

- Broadcast and multicast with a satellite overlay
- Internet of Things with a satellite network
- Temporary use of a satellite component
- Optimal routing or steering over a satellite
- Satellite transborder service continuity
- Global satellite overlay
- Indirect connection through a 5G satellite access network
- 5G Fixed Backhaul between NR and the 5G Core
- 5G Moving Platform Backhaul
- 5G to Premises
- Satellite connection of remote service center to offshore wind farm

3.2.2 Proposed system architectures

To provide service connectivity to the use cases described in Section 3.2.1, several architecture options [10] have been discussed during the 5G standardization process carried out within 3GPP and also further developed by industry and academia in projects and related research investigations. More specifically, classical satellite backhaul is complemented by direct access to satellite, with the former essentially consisting of transparently interconnecting a 5G terrestrial-based RAN to *the 5G Core Network (CN)* by means of a satellite system. On the other hand, the latter relates to the possibility to deploy an actual satellite RAN, which can be seen as a standalone 5G entity implementation or operating in coordination with a terrestrial RAN to optimally provide connectivity means towards the already mentioned scenarios of service continuity and ubiquity. As a consequence of these architectural options, a significant set of key issues are to be considered in the design of an integrated NTN-5G (and beyond system), such as:

- Mobility management with large and/or moving satellite coverage areas.
- Role of delay in satellites.
- QoS management with satellite access and backhaul.
- RAN mobility with *non-geostationary Orbit (NGSO)* regenerative-based satellite access.
- Multi-connectivity with satellite access and hybrid satellite/terrestrial backhaul.
- The role of satellite link in content distribution towards the Edge.
- Regulatory services with super-national satellite ground station.

In relation to the above key issues, two general architecture implementations are in turn proposed, namely, direct and indirect access. The former implies direct connectivity from UEs to satellites (or in a broad sense NTNs), whereas the latter considers the insertion of a relay node acting as a repeater at L1/L2 between satellite and UEs. These two options are then in turn further subdivided in dependence on the specific satellite platform implementation, that is, transparent vs. regenerative. In the case of transparent satellite, a gNB is typically placed by a satellite hub, so that NR signal distribution happens from UE to gNB over the satellite link, with the due adaptations necessary to account for the satellite link peculiarities (e.g., larger, and variable delay, important Doppler effects, etc.). On the other hand, the case of regenerative satellite payload opens the door to the implementation of a gNB onboard satellite, whereby NR signal distribution is achieved only over the satellite user link. Then, the signal is propagated to the 5G CN over the satellite radio interface of the feeder link or through inter-satellite links, as envisioned for future LEO constellations. Notably, the implementation of gNB nodes onboard satellite is becoming an attractive option and possibly considered for the Rel. 19 of 3GPP RAN, though important architectural and protocol investigations are still to be carried out. In particular, the implementation of a full gNB in space is not so straightforward because of the limited resource availability onboard satellites, so that the consolidated *centralized unit-distributed unit (CU-DU)* splitting approach for achieving a modular implementation of gNB in terrestrial networks is considered appealing also for forthcoming satellite systems. Still in this case, however, some open point relates to the actual feasibility of DU functionalities implementation in space, given the fact that they are typically resources-hangry, which must be validated against the power and computation budget limits typically experienced by the present satellite systems.

Another relevant scenario emerging from the integration of NTN into 5G/6G systems is the support for multi-connectivity scenarios as well as the management of mobility [11]. As to the former, it mostly relates to the possible capability of simultaneously exploiting satellite and terrestrial links from UEs to the 5G CN, which implies proper design choices, especially in relation to the gNB functional implementation. On the other hand, mobility management plays an important role especially in the case of NGSO satellite systems interconnecting UEs to 5G CNs, in that their limited visibility introduces handover events, which may result in switching from one gNB to another or in any case to feeder link switching, whose operations pretty much depend on the adopted architecture option (direct vs. indirect access) and on the satellite configuration (transparent vs. regenerative, with the latter possibly implementing a full gNB or the related DU functionalities).

An additional option of possible future exploitation, though not considered as part of 3GPP Rel. 17 of NTN systems, is the case of *integrated-access and backhaul (IAB)*, which has become quite mature for 5G wireless terrestrial systems. Its attractiveness stems mostly from the possibility of reusing resources across access and backhaul links, which is certainly a desired optimal configuration in satellite systems. There are however still important challenges to be completely understood especially in relation to the overall applicability of the IAB architecture concepts (e.g., IAB-donor for satellite systems) and the actual feasibility of using the IAB protocol in space, which may suffer from the larger latencies in comparison to those typically experienced in terrestrial networks.

3.3 Key Technical Challenges

3.3.1 Network orchestration

Network orchestration is a central element of the service-oriented architecture adopted for the deployment of 5G and future generations of cellular communications. Owing to the full network softwarization, support the distribution of network functions in dedicated modules that are implemented according to the *network function virtualization (NFV)* paradigm and hence allow automatic network reconfiguration to meet the requirements of the verticals making use of such a service architecture. As such, the network orchestration becomes the central element, able to glue together the user with the control plane functions and hence provide connectivity to users throughout RAN and core network. The problem of effective network orchestration is already particularly challenging in current terrestrial 5G networks, because of the coexistence of standalone and non-standalone 5G deployments as well as the presence of multiple operators managing a different portion of the same communication network, whereby a purely central approach is not feasible. The design of an effective network orchestration paradigm becomes even more complex in the case of integrated NTN-terrestrial networks [13], in that terrestrial and non-terrestrial segment exhibit very different characteristics and historically different network management models have been developed in isolation. As such, the case of an integrated satellite-terrestrial network where multiple satellite and cellular operators act on the different parts of the end-to-end infrastructure in a segregated manner introduces some key challenges in the design of an efficient orchestration mechanism. In particular, the possibility of a centralized orchestrator is less attractive and on the contrary, the concept of a cross-domain orchestrator is becoming more and more appealing. Then a possible approach is to come up with a multi-layered network orchestration architecture, so that micro network orchestrators are responsible for restricted network areas and coordination amongst them is achieved by means of higher-level orchestration. Even so, however, there are still important open research questions in relation to the management of satellite networks once integrated into terrestrial ones, which may introduce important fluctuations in the connectivity, whereby classical network management approaches are not any longer viable. On the contrary, closer cooperation across all parts of the entire network is necessary for the envisaged network orchestrator to collect the information necessary to carry out timely decisions. Given the fact, that key elements of network orchestration, such as mobility management, network slicing, service function chaining depend on many parameters, coming up with a close-form optimal mathematical solution is in general not possible. On the contrary, the application of federated learning principles throughout the integrated network are emerging as particularly promising thanks to their capability to let network operators to track the time/space dynamics of data traffic flow and then ultimately let networks to self-reconfigure.

3.3.2 Network slicing

Network slicing is a key component of 5G and future 6G network architectures, with a strong interaction with the functionalities envisioned in the network orchestrator. More specifically, this paradigm is fundamental to simultaneously fulfill the possibly diverse QoS requirements demanded by the verticals subscribing to the 5G/6G transport network services. Network slicing essentially partitions the available physical network infrastructure into a set of logical network slices, characterized by several service functions which are chained together in order to offer the demanded performance. Each service function is then directly linked to classical tasks such as management of energy consumption, caching, edge computing, and resource allocation, which are in turn implemented by dedicated agents of the network protocol stack. Deep utilization of SDN and NFV concepts obviously plays an important role toward the automatization of such mechanisms and hence their adaptation to the network dynamics, in terms of traffic variations, channel quality fluctuations, etc., just to cite a few. Such a dynamic network slicing management is of key importance also in the deployment of current and future 6G-NTN networks [14], where the variety of space assets and the seamless integration to the terrestrial counterpart gives shape to a very diverse communication environment in terms of data transfer capabilities. The specific adaptation of network slicing mechanisms to the network dynamics is therefore strictly dependent on the many degrees of freedom possibly influencing the overall end-to-end system behavior. In this respect, the establishment or the update of network slices must undergo continuous monitoring and periodic optimization in order to tune the slice configurations to the observed network status while still meeting QoS verticals' demands. The need for such a mechanism is already straightforward in "simple" satellite systems (e.g., standalone) where regenerative payload may allow for power and bandwidth allocation, which should be tuned also according to LEO constellation handover events or more general traffic fluctuations. Obviously, in the case of multi-connected satellite systems, the number of degrees of freedom increases substantially so that defining adequate network slices is a challenging problem, which must be addressed in an optimal manner on wider scale (not just at physical level at satellite level, but throughout the entire communication network). Such an optimization approach is however not just about classical QoS management but more importantly, entails the placement and related chaining of the key service functions to attain a certain level of desired QoS. Such a task becomes prohibitive in multi-orbit NTN networks integrated with terrestrial where the non-continuous availability of data connectivity as well as the possible need for data offloading from terrestrial to NTN networks and vice versa requires a proper observe-and-control optimization loop, which eventually results in a multi-dimensional multi-objective optimization problem which can be hardly solved by means of classical approaches. To cope with such an increase in complexity, the aid of AI-based approaches, such as deep learning also deployed in a heavily distributed manner is fundamental to track the network dynamics variations and hence take the proper decision on the available network slices.

3.3.3 Edge computing

Edge computing as well as the broader in-network computation paradigms are receiving quite some interest from the satellite community in that elaboration of huge amount of data (resulting from IoT or *earth observation (EO)* imaging services) directly at the processing center is too much time-consuming and overall burdensome. As such, some studies have been already carried out [15], to figure out the possible application of Edge computing concepts directly in space, by exploiting the available computation capabilities of satellites. So far, the developed system architecture is pretty much purpose-driven, so that no specific interoperability needs with other existing systems or architecture are considered. Nevertheless, the next step is to have Edge computing architecture implemented onboard satellites in a way that they are compliant with ETSI MEC specifications. More importantly, the next frontier would be to combine Edge computing concepts with regenerative satellite payloads in a general 5G (and later 6G) oriented architecture, wherein the satellite infrastructure will implement a full gNB also inclusive of the User Plane Functions (UPF). Under this perspective, important technical challenges relate to defining a network architecture enabling edge computing service provisioning to users. As such, service discovery, mapping of users to micro-services, as well as general resource allocation are key questions to be answered to achieve an effective edge computing system design. Moreover, edge computing is to be seen as distributed across multiple space assets as well as terrestrial nodes, whereby networking challenges arising from network and users' mobility require proper understanding to identify the main functional requirements driving the design of such a complex integrated system. Last but not the least, an important role here will be again played by AI to support distributed and collaborative task execution across multiple nodes. Conversely, edge computing can also be seen as enabler for carrying out AI in space, especially for all tasks necessitating some advanced data processing as soon as data are being generated (i.e., onboard satellites).

3.3.4 Routing

Routing is a key functionality in mesh networks, as envisioned in the case of future NTN systems, where multiple space assets will be interconnected by means of links exhibiting very diverse characteristics. In particular, network mobility with respect to the users on the ground, frequent handover events, as well as the related QoS management makes the adoption of classical routing schemes as those deployed in terrestrial systems not adequate. In this respect, more advanced techniques building on both geographic [16] and semantic concepts are necessary for complex NTN networks to provide adaptive and flexible connectivity means to the final users. In particular, the possibly evolving network topology in space and time along with the variation of data traffic requires the exploitation of multi-path concepts and the capability of space nodes to promptly react to possible congestion events and therefore carry out offloading or re-routing operations by still fulfilling specific QoS requirements. Such a complex decision-making approach can be regarded as a multi-dimensional multi-objective optimization framework that can be hardly approached by means of analytic solutions or in general through traditional numerical methods. On the contrary, more attention has been taken in the last years to the possible adoption of AI-based mechanisms to provide routing agents with the necessary information about network topology change and traffic variations (just to cite some of the possible degrees of freedom) and eventually let take the optima decisions. Obviously, the application of AI-based schemes is becoming even more compelling in dense satellite constellations, whereby distributed learning mechanisms are necessary and proper coordination amongst all the routing agents is of paramount importance to guarantee the definition of a QoS-compliant path for the data flows to be routed.

3.3.5 Resource allocation

Resource allocation in NTN systems is becoming again a hot topic [17] given the important advances in satellite system design with respect to the capabilities possibly offered by the flexible payload. In particular, the capability of dynamically allocating power, frequency, and/or time according to traffic fluctuations jointly combined with optimized beamforming is one of the recent trends in the design of satellite communication systems. This aspect can be also coupled with the increasing interest to use of *non-orthogonal multiple access (NOMA)* principles in satellite systems. Overall, the problem of resource allocation is strongly influenced by the interference mitigation/avoidance schemes necessary to cope with interference caused by the various links possibly interconnecting the several space assets of a 3D NTN network. This becomes even more stringent when opportunistic spectrum reuse across terrestrial and non-terrestrial networks is exploited, hence requiring proper coordination and effective resource allocation schemes. In this respect, the exploitation of AI techniques is an absolute need, given the fact that the many degrees of freedom make the problem of optimal resource allocation computationally unfeasible in terms of classical or analytical approaches. This problem has been recently addressed for the case of GEO satellite systems and is certainly more crucial and challenging in NGSO satellite constellations where traffic variability in space and time, the distribution nature of the network connectivity, as well as the possible handover events, makes the optimization problem very complicated. In such a case, quite some attention is not only dedicated to the specific flavor of AI to be used but also to how to properly distribute AI-based agents according to federated learning principle to achieve optimal resource allocation. As such, the solution of the optimization problem through AI schemes introduces some important network architecture implications as to where such computation capabilities should be placed in a global network and how should be the results of the decision-making process communicated to network nodes to carry out the corresponding resource allocation actions.

3.4 Future Directions

3.4.1 New technology development

The need for hyper-connectivity is hence requiring close integration between ground and space subsystems as argued in the previous sections of this survey, which is eventually the key point for including NTN technologies into the 6G technology ecosystem. Despite the possible exploitation of AI paradigms applied together with deep network programmability concepts, offering unprecedented capacity even to remote users is strictly depending on the available technology at physical layer (i.e., antennas and related use of frequency bands), which may open or conversely constrain the upper bound of the available data rate. In this light, some efforts have been already done in the rest past to achieve the so-called concept of terabit satellites, which eventually results in the conception of the so-called ultra-high throughput satellites offering an overall satellite capacity in the order of Terabit/s. To achieve such a capacity, the considered approach was to exploit Ka-band also in the user link and possibly migrate the feeder link to higher frequency bands such as Q/V or even W, to make use of larger portions of those frequency bands which are presently not much used. This comes, however, at higher costs in terms of network deployment because of the necessity of implementing space-diversity concepts to cope with possibly frequent feeder link outages. Such an ambitious design has pushed the satellite community (academia and industry) to come up with the so-called concept of smart-gateway diversity that naturally brings some important challenges at antenna and resource allocation design level as well as in terms of the networking functionalities needed to guarantee proper levels of QoS throughout the integrated terrestrial-satellite network.

An additional approach considered in this context is to complement Q/V band- or W band-based feeder link with a new generation of gateways equipped with *free-space optics (FSO)* transceivers [18], possibly offering a much higher data rate (in the order of a few tens of Gbit/s) in comparison to the RF counterpart. Such an opportunity has been attracting considerably the research community and industry because of the new market slices that can be taken from the satellite industry, but the technology is still considered not fully mature for an actual mass productization process. From a technical standpoint, this is mostly due to the fact that feeder links building on FSO technology are quite prone to link outages caused by atmospheric impairments (e.g., Clouds), whereby more sophisticated system design is necessary at slightly higher costs in terms of deployments. Possible strategies here relate to the use of adaptive optics in the design of the telescope, making use of long-interleavers, or even resorting to packet-layer coding solutions to cope with possible link interruptions. More importantly, long interruptions must be then mitigated by means of redundant gateways and possibly by *delay/disruption tolerant networking (DTN)* concepts so that it is possible to intelligently switch data communication from one gateway to an alternate one.

The exploitation of FSO is not only relevant for achieving the aforementioned concept of Terabits satellites, but in general for "extending" the fiber optics-based network into space and allowing to achieve the so-called high-speed data highway in space. The original concept consists of interconnecting EO-based LEO satellites to GEO ones through FSO ISLs, which is the baseline of the *European data relay service (EDRS)*. Further to that, more recently ESA has started the *HyDRON (high throughput optical network)*[1] initiative, which is really aimed at interconnecting ground infrastructure with space assets by means of a mesh network mostly building on FSO in space. This has the benefit of exploiting the large data rate intrinsically offered by FSO links on the one hand and taking advantage of lower-delay links for connecting very far apart areas (i.e., intercontinental connections), which would necessitate several hops through the terrestrial infrastructure in-land and then across submarine cables. On the contrary, exploitation of mesh networks in space allows connecting remote areas more flexibly one with another through a limited number of hop and with possibly lower latency, in virtue of the fact that light speed in space is higher than that measured in cables (e.g., fiber optics). Integration of such complex networks requires however an additional effort in understanding all implications at the physical layer and network design, as shortly outlined in the next subsection.

---

[1] https://artes.esa.int/funding/high-throughput-optical-network-hydron-scylight-sl021.

3.4.2 Additional research areas

As overviewed in the previous subsection, several technology developments are ongoing, which will have an important impact on the effective integration of terrestrial and non-terrestrial networks. Certainly, the vision of a hyper-connected space domain through assets at different orbits and offering communication capabilities through different technologies open the discussion to many intriguing research questions. On the one hand, such a complex environment will exhibit important fluctuations in the overall service latency, variations of the available data rates, as well as frequent handover events. As such, traditional network architecture based on IP may not scale well in space, whereby dedicated solutions could be more effective. Obviously, key point to be addressed is whether the deployment of dedicated network protocols is actually feasible, given the fact that the rest of the network architecture will still rely on IP-based technology, hence necessitating proper convergence between IP and non-IP domains. A possible workaround could be then to resort on higher layer solutions (i.e., possibly functioning on top of IP) to keep backward compatibility with IP products, which would be then required to expose the necessary function interface to interwork with overlaying architectures. These latter would then be responsible for more advanced multi-path and handover strategies, as somehow already proposed with the cases of DTN and ICN solutions and related variants circulated during the last decade.

Additional points of investigation relate to the applicability of some of the trends currently considered in wireless terrestrial system such as *reconfigurable intelligent surfaces (RIS)* [19] or THz-based satellite systems. In both cases, no specific results or conclusions are already available since deeper investigations are needed to understand the actual value these technologies can bring in the overall SatCom context and to also figure out if the maturity of electronic components available now may enable such utilization. This is particularly the case of THz communications, requiring electronic components not currently available for use in space.

Last but not the least, the increasing interest toward quantum technologies has certainly exerted a non-negligible influence also on the visionary programs of satellite systems evolution. If on the one hand, the case *of quantum key distribution (QKD)* has been quite considerably analyzed for use in satellite communication systems, the broader context of quantum communication systems (also including computing) is still not fully part of the satellite communication evolution agenda and more specific studies have to be carried out in this regard to understand primarily the feasibility of running quantum network offering also quantum computing capabilities where integrated satellite and terrestrial network segments are envisioned.

3.5 Conclusion

This chapter surveyed the main directions taken from research and industry toward the unification of terrestrial and non-terrestrial network ecosystems so as to achieve a more effective and sustainable 6G deployment concept. In this respect, the adoption within non-terrestrial systems of technologies firmly employed in terrestrial infrastructures since a couple of years such as Cloud-RAN, network slicing, edge computing, and network softwarization has determined an important design shift, considered fundamental for the integration with the terrestrial infrastructures. There are however still formidable challenges in the full adoption of key 5G-native technologies because of the unique peculiarities of NTN systems, in terms of mobility and overall network management. From this standpoint, the paper importantly outlined the increasing interest in the satellite community toward regenerative satellite payload to provide a more varied set of services, possibly being offered directly from the satellite platform. From this perspective, NTN infrastructures are expected to be integrated into the rest of the 6G ecosystem in the form of *"infrastructure-as-a-service"*, where the specific services possibly offered depend on the satellite system characterization and the overall functionalities therein made available. Despite the continuous increase of interest towards the integration of NTN into 6G, there are still important aspects to be further investigated especially in relation to business models able to capture the demand/offer dynamics of integrated terrestrial and satellite systems. Furthermore, another important aspect is the actual adaptivity of the satellite industry with respect to terrestrial counterpart, to allow for seamless convergence and eventually shape the playground for a cooperative 6G system development.

References

[1] Study on Using Satellite Access in 5G, Version 16.0.0, Release 16, Standard TR 22.822.2018, 3GPP, 2020.

[2] K. Xue et al., "Guest Editorial: Space Information Networks: Technological Challenges, Design Issues, and Solutions," in IEEE Network, vol. 35, no. 4, pp. 16-18, July/August 2021.

[3] Thomas Heyn; Alexander Hofmann; Sahana Raghunandan; Leszek Raschkowski, "Non-Terrestrial Networks in 6G," in Shaping Future 6G Networks: Needs, Impacts, and Technologies , IEEE, 2022, pp. 101-116, doi: 10.1002/9781119765554.ch8.

[4] S. Liu et al., "LEO Satellite Constellations for 5G and Beyond: How Will They Reshape Vertical Domains?," in IEEE Communications Magazine, vol. 59, no. 7, pp. 30-36, July 2021.

[5] A. Guidotti et al., "Architectures and Key Technical Challenges for 5G Systems Incorporating Satellites," in IEEE Transactions on Vehicular Technology, vol. 68, no. 3, pp. 2624-2639, March 2019.

4

Cognitive Service-centric Satellite Networks

Paulo M. Mendes

Airbus Central Research
E-mail: paulo.mendes@airbus.com

Abstract

Several companies have been investing significantly in new LEO satellite constellations to provide Internet access anywhere on Earth, while satellite operators aim to combine GEO with NGSO systems. In this scenario, a global network of a large number of satellites aims to sustain seamless connectivity enabling access around the globe, which is an essential humanitarian need. The increasingly demand for Internet connectivity everywhere and anytime highlights the need to rethink about a suitable way to manage large-scale networks, as is the case of multi-orbit satellite constellations. This chapter aims to analyze a set of design choices to devise a suitable networking framework able to sustain the operation of dynamic network services in large-scale multi-orbit satellite constellations.

Keywords: Satellite Constellation, Space Internet, Service-centric Networking, Cognitive Networking.

4.1 Introduction

The telecommunication industry has consistently endeavored to provide high throughput and low latency when it comes to connectivity solutions. In the meantime, satellite technologies have been playing a significant role in providing global communication services.

The need for expanding Internet access to a truly global system is being obvious during the COVID-19 pandemic, which is forcing the world to

31

embrace a fully digital society. However, the high cost of building terrestrial infrastructures is a key barrier in providing ubiquitous broadband Internet access. In this context, the required global Internet access can be achieved via the integration of terrestrial and satellite networks. Historically dominated by GEO technology, the satellite communication market is now embracing LEO satellite technology. Moreover, the exploitation of LEO technology can be combined with the development of multi-orbit systems, where operators combine GEO with NGSO systems to provide their customers with the best networking experience: constellations in LEO or *medium earth orbit (MEO)* offering low-latency connectivity, and GEO satellites providing more capacity around the entire globe. However, there are several potential factors that may limit the access to have to Internet services via satellite constellations. Hence, this chapter starts by introducing large-scale satellite networks and a set of deployment choices to ensure a truly global access to such networks. Driven by the vision of a truly global Internet access able to support emerging services, such as autonomous vehicles, tactile Internet, and metaverse, there is the need to support a more flexible, scalable, and low-cost operation of large-scale satellite networks. In this context, this chapter tackles a set of architecture design choices needed to devise a suitable networking framework able to sustain large-scale networks, while still following the network automation path envisioned for 6G networks. Such a networking framework aims to allow large-scale satellite networks to become cognitive by observing and acting autonomously to optimize the performance of flexible network services. Besides the usage of AI to furnish the needed automation and prediction, the envisioned networking framework needs to be able to interact with a variety of network technologies, such as host agnostic networking, network slicing, semantic network operations, traffic aware service management, as well as the convergence of optical transport and routing functionality. Since it will be difficult to manage flexible and fine-grained end-to-end services with the current architecture of mobile networks and satellite networks, this chapter aims to help in redesigning future large-scale satellite networks to achieve a powerful, flexible, and intelligent networking experience, while seamlessly integrating with terrestrial networks.

4.2 Large-scale Satellite Networks

Over the last several years, the world has witnessed a resurgent interest in space-based Internet services, particularly with mega-constellations of LEO satellites such as Starlink, Amazon, Telesat, and OneWeb. LEO satellites are located approximately 50 times closer to Earth, offering low latency (less than 30ms), and relatively high throughput (approximately 100 Mbps) in comparison to GEO satellites (c.f., Figure 4.1).

Moreover, internetworking with GEO may allow LEO constellations to route traffic between different geographic areas, avoiding busy areas, while internetworking with *high-altitude platform systems (HAPS)* may compensate for local outages of some part of the LEO constellation. Such multi-orbit satellite networks have the potential to mitigate the existent digital divide, based on its global footprint, which must be achieved based on low costs and seamless interoperability. To cut costs, satellite operators aim to reduce the number of ground stations, meaning that satellites need be able to form a space network, supported by *inter-satellite links (ISL)* based on FSO technology. FSO links have a low cost and allow space networks to achieve low end-to-end delays since free-space lasers communicate at the speed of light in a vacuum, which is circa 47% higher than fiber [16]. The cost of satellite networks can also be reduced by integrating them with terrestrial networks. Although 5G was designed to target terrestrial communications without considering satellite access, efforts have been made to adapt 5G systems to support satellite communications. It is expected users to have access to cellular devices with NTN support, allowing roaming between cellular and satellite networks seamlessly [13], or even to have multi-homed devices. Allowing users to have simultaneous and transparent access to more than one network provider, possibly based on different technology (e.g.,

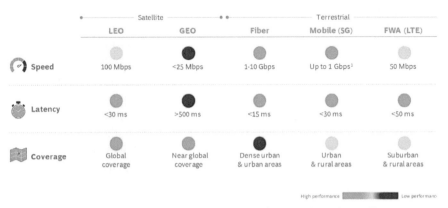

Figure 4.1 Performance of LEO satellites.

space and cellular), will boost service reliability. On the same page, such diversity should also be included in the core of the Internet where network paths via a space Internet should be included alongside submarine cables allowing to reduce the dependence upon any specific technology, as well as the companies and countries behind it. The realization of such a multi-connected networking scenario based on the combination of satellite and terrestrial networks will be a challenge based on current *Internet Protocol (IP)* technologies. Such challenge comes due to some inefficiencies of the current Internet architecture to support large-scale mobile networks with intermittent connectivity. The root of these inefficiencies relates with the fact that the Internet current host-centric communication model does not allow information to be exchanged independently of the location of the device holding the information.

4.3 Internetworking Challenge and 6G Alignment

Independently of the used topology, a satellite network may be based on a non-regenerative or a regenerative platform. The former is commonly called "bent-pipe," since the satellite does not terminate any networking layers. On the other hand, regenerative payloads, also called *on-board processing (OBP)*, provide additional functionality based on the capability of terminating one or more layers of the protocol stack. This capability allows the internet-working of the satellite system with IP networks below the IP layer (bridge internetworking function), at the IP layer (IP internetworking function), and above the IP layer (gateway function). The operation of large-scale satellite networks requires OBP platforms able to implement at least layer 3 of the IP protocol stack. The first IP stack was installed on board of the UoSAT-12 satellite built by Surrey Satellite Technology Ltd (SSTL) in 2000, while the Cisco *Internet Routing in Space (IRIS)* project (2009) provided the ability to route IP traffic to onboard a satellite. The ability to process IP traffic in space helps reduce end-to-end delays and increase the network capacity, while enabling flexible bandwidth-on-demand services without any static configuration. Forwarding IP traffic in space faces the challenge of dealing with the intermittent connectivity of the satellite system, which can be tackled by using DTNs [34]. In this context, the DTN bundle protocol [18] was ported to SSTL on-board computers allowing chaining of different TCP sessions between custodian satellites to achieve end-to-end connectivity over a set of intermittently connected satellites. From a routing perspective, data exchange is rather challenging in such networks since paths between any pair of nodes may never exist or delay may be too long to be accepted by current transport protocols. There are nevertheless already a significant number of proposals to opportunistically route data based on time-variant graphs used by DTN [24], each with a different goal and based on different evaluation criteria [25]. Other constraints of the first generation of IP routers in space were power consumption and the lack of capability to be remotely managed while in operation. Overcoming these limitations requires an IP networking solution based on a zero-touch deployment approach aiming to allow the update of software functionality and the installation of novel technical solutions. Hence, a successful internetworking of terrestrial and non-terrestrial networks requires the evolution toward a true end-to-end service-based architecture flexible enough to handle the dynamic behavior of satellite networks and able of supporting new services and capabilities [17]. Hence, this chapter argues in favor of the development of a service-based network architecture able of controlling end-to-end services defined by aggregating networking, storage, and computational resources, and orchestrated based on operational intents. Being aligned with a 6G vision [9], such architecture encompasses a set of new functionalities, such as address space customization, data integrity and authentication, in-network storage and computing, semantic forwarding and routing, and automation of traffic engineering and service management functions.

4.4 Towards Service-centric Satellite Networks

There is currently renewed interest in the role of satellites within next-generation wireless networks, such as 6G. In 6G networks, an integrated terrestrial – NTN network can address gaps that currently exist in terrestrial networks. Services carried over such integrated network is expected to cover broadband services, mobile backhaul, IoT, and *vehicle-to-everything*. However, data transmission over satellites has historically experienced long delays, affecting mostly delay-sensitive services. The deployment of LEO satellites helps mitigate this limitation. However, each LEO satellite covers a reduced area on the ground, meaning that a high number of satellites are required to provide global coverage, in which case satellites need to be able to route traffic between different parts of the space network. To support the envisioned set of future services, besides being able to route traffic within the space network, there is the need to devise intelligent and flexible networking solutions able to support not only packet switching, but also data storage and processing, while being able to react in real time to the requirements of new operational intents. Such future satellite network aims to reduce data rate requirements, increase energy efficiency, and guarantee end-to-end network connectivity. Therefore, a new network architecture for large-scale multi-orbit satellite systems should be able to abstract a set of networking, storage, and computing resources in the form of end-to-end services, deployed to fulfill a set of operational intents that may change over time. To sustain a large set of services, the envisioned network architecture should rely on a programmable data plane, flexible enough to support different services based on a chain of virtual network functions, such as distinct forwarding mechanisms. From an end-to-end perspective, there is the need to develop routing strategies able to consider different service semantics (e.g., load balancing), as well as to exploit a mesh of FSO links. This goal may require converging the optical transport with the routing functionality, increasing power efficiency, and scalability.

4.4.1 Service-centric networking

The architectural approach used on the Internet is inherited from the host-centric approach used in the telephone network, based on the general same idea: the network connects two networked devices, identified by a pair of host addresses that are used to establish and control a connectivity. Since the creation of the Internet traffic volume has grown considerably being expected to reach nearly 400 billion GB in 2022 [4]. Since the Internet is still growing, not only in terms of traffic but also covered with the integration of NTN and terrestrial networks, there is the need to investigate suitable alternative network architectures. One of the most prominent future Internet architectures is ICN [7], *named data networking (NDN)* [37] a prominent ICN implementation. ICN forwards packets based on data identifiers instead of host identifiers. This shifts the current host-centric Internet paradigm towards a new data-centric approach. ICN enables a consumer to request a given data object from the network without any knowledge about the location of the requested data.

This paradigm shift brings several benefits to the operation of large-scale satellite networks, namely the adaptation to intermittent connected links [6] based on a pull communication model and in-network caching, as well as extra flexibility to handle different types of traffic, based on an extended set of forwarding strategies. While some analysis about the development of ICN-based satellite systems has been made [31], some new ICN-based architectures have been proposed to support a universal networking system able to encompass spaceborne and airborne platforms [30]. Although a data-centric approach reflects better the current operation of the Internet, services are an essential component of its operation: users request services rather than data. Services are pieces of software that can be remotely called and executed using an underlying network infrastructure. A service is usually offered by a remote service provider and is requested by a service consumer: the communication between the service provider and service consumer is enabled by a service-based naming scheme. Hence, there is the need to extend ICN to support a network operation based on services and not on data objects. Such service-centric architecture should not alter the ICN primitives used to create its pull communication model but should instead extend it to support services that are seen by the network as software functions that can be requested by service consumers. There are several proposals aiming to extend ICN to devise a service-centric network architecture. In general, all of them handle service requests as illustrated in Figure 4.2. In this example, a client wants to compress a file and then encrypt it with a password given by a selected function. In this example, ICN routers forward the client request to a service replica offering the encrypt function (1). Upon receiving the service request, the encrypt function parses the parameters from the Interest message and sends a service request for a compression function (2). The request is again forwarded as a traditional ICN Interest. Upon receiving the request, the compression function parses it and sends a request to gather the file indicated in the request (3). When the compression function receives the file (4), it compresses it and sends the result back to the encrypt function (5), which encrypts the compressed file with the password that in the meantime retreated from a local function and sends the result as an ICN data message to the service requester (6). There are several proposals to extend *content-centric networking (CCN)*, an ICN flavor, to support services namely CCNxServ [8]; NextServe [22]; and *Named Function Networking (NFN)* [33]. Nevertheless, CCNxServ has many limitations, namely forcing services to be delivered in one single file, and not fully complying with the CCN architecture. NextServe leverages CCN based on the notion of service composition with function chaining. However, NextServe inherits CCNxServ limitations and does not integrate load-balancing support. Load balancing is supported by NFN, which can redirect service requests to neighboring nodes if a service provider is overloaded. However, the NFN-naming scheme, based on lambda expression, is hard to read especially when there are multiple function calls.

Named function as a service (NFaaS) [20] is another dynamic in-network-computing approach like NFN but based on NDN. Trying to mitigate the

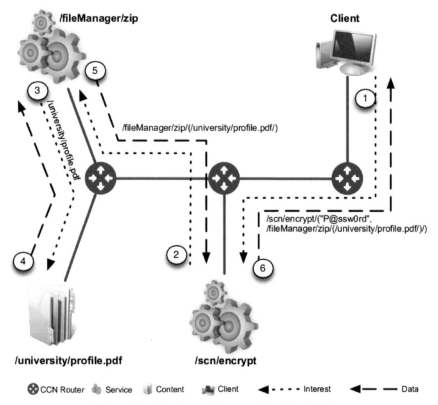

Figure 4.2 Service-centric request handling [22].

NFN limitations, NFaaS uses hierarchical naming and unikernels functions instead of lambda expressions. One of the major limitations of NFaaS is that the execution of functions can generate a lot of traffic and delay because functions must be downloaded prior to execution. Based on this analysis, a suitable service-centric network architecture should support any type of input parameter, relying on ICN primitives, as well as load balancing of service requests (c.f., Section 4.4.4).

4.4.2 Programmable networks

In order to sustain a diversified set of services, a suitable communication data plane should be flexible enough to support the specific requirements of different services, each of which can require for instance a distinct forwarding mechanism. In a service-centric architecture, such a data plane uses location-independent service identifiers. In order to support a service-oriented operation of the network, hosts should be allowed to insert the identifier of the desired service(s) into the appropriate packet header field, making it possible for routers and/or switches to make forwarding decisions based on the service identifier in the packet header. However, although the control plane of traditional networking devices such as routers and switches can be configurable (e.g., via CLIs or management APIs), the underlying data plane can only be changed by the equipment vendor. This limitation has been mitigated by the *software-defined networking (SDN)* paradigm and even more by programable data planes. The softwarization of the data plan allows for instance network traffic to be forwarded through different virtual machines running on commodity CPUs. This approach simplifies the development of network programs without relying on proprietary network processors. On the one hand, SDN makes network devices programmable by introducing an API that allows users to bypass the built-in control plane and replace it with customized algorithms that run on an SDN controller, which may have an overall view of the network. Such an overall view of the network allows complex-distributed control algorithms to be replaced by simpler algorithms designed for centralized usage. On the other hand, programmable data planes enable users to implement their own data plane algorithms on forwarding devices. For instance, network operators may define new protocol headers and forwarding behavior, which is without programmable data plane can only be deployed by the equipment vendor. Such programmable data plan may also encompass extended APIs for SDN control. There are different data plane programming models, each with many implementations and programming languages, such as *vector packet processing (VPP)* [1], and SDNet [35]. An emerging approach in programming software switches is by defining the operation of the data plane through a *domain-specific language (DSL)*, such as P4 [21], and then compiling it to a program that interacts with the interfaces available on the target software router/switch. However, there are challenges in compiling the data plane program efficiently, especially if the equipment only exposes a limited set of interfaces for the definition of the runtime behavior. Hence, a programmable data plan should expose an extended set of interfaces besides the ones used to specify high-level forwarding behavior, as is the case of the VPP framework. The VPP framework exposes a set of low-level primitives that can interact directly with the CPU and has a unique node graph packet processing model where a vector of packets is processed through a series of processing nodes, each using a different set of instructions. Nevertheless, programming VPP is challenging precisely due to its complex organization and the amount of tuning required to obtain acceptable performance. PVPP [3] alleviates this by compiling a data plane program specified in P4 to code that executes within VPP. Thus, the programmer is allowed to express the desired data plane features through a friendly match-action abstraction.

4.4.3 Semantic routing

Large-scale satellite networks aim to transfer large volumes of data between tens of thousands of satellites that move continuously at high speeds in different orbits. To support this aim, there is a need to develop new protocols for routing traffic from different services. Such protocols can leverage existing solutions to route data over a large set of mobile devices, based on specific algorithms such as Contact Graph Routing [12] as well as ICN [23]. Modern networks are designed to carry traffic belonging to different services with distinct specifications in terms of traffic performance, reliability, and robustness [14]. However, the continuous motion of satellites poses significant difficulties to traditional routing protocols. For instance, as satellite constellations become very large, the routing may never fully converge, resulting in a suboptimal network. Moreover, there is the need to develop routing strategies able to consider different service semantics described by a combination of fields in the packet header as well as a transported set of instructions. Such routing strategies require a data plan able to support programmable network functions (e.g., forwarding) and services as described in Section 4.4.2. Semantic routing is the process of achieving enhanced decisions based on semantics added to IP headers aiming to provide differentiated paths for different services. The additional information or" semantics" may be placed in existing header fields (e.g., the IPv6 Traffic Class field), may be added to new header fields, or it may be encoded in the payload or on additional headers, such as the IPv6 Extension Header.

The application of semantic routing allows packets from different services to be marked for different treatments in the network. The packets may then be routed onto different paths according to the capabilities and states of the network links and nodes, to meet the performance requirements. For example, one service may need low latency, while another may require ultra-low jitter, and a third may demand very high bandwidth. Examples of existing semantic routing usage in IP-based networks include i) using addresses to identify different device types so that their traffic may be handled differently [32]; ii) expressing how a packet should be handled as it is forwarded through the network [36]; iii) enable *service function chaining (SFC)* [15]; iv) forwarding packets based on carried data rather than the destination addresses [28]; v) or formatting geographic location information within addresses [5]. SFC is an essential concept for the development of a service-centric architecture, in the same sense that "network slicing" was applied to the specific case of 5G networks. SFC is applied at the network layer to steer packet flows through network functions, such as security, load balancing, or even DTN custodians: service chains are sequence of service instances (network functions). Packets are tunneled between service instances using encapsulation, by using techniques such as the *network service header (NSH)* [26] or segment routing, which may be more widely applicable based on programmable data planes (c.f., Section 4.4.2). Any semantic routing solution encompasses three phases: i) discover the capabilities and state of network links and nodes; ii) mark packets with semantic information according to their required delivery characteristics; and iii) program routers to forward traffic according to how the packets are marked. An example is the explicit service-based IP routing [2] that abstracts service instances into several classes called *service action types (SATs)*. Each packet is marked with the relevant SAT, and packets are routed to the next available SAT provider instead of to the destination IP address. A sequence of SAT to be followed by a packet can be included in the packet header, similarly to what happens with segment routing: this can be done based on P4 by introducing a header that contains segments that identify each operation, for example, forwarding the packet to the next available SAT provider. Network nodes process packets according to the topmost segment in the segment routing header and remove it after successful execution. An applicability case for semantic routing in large-scale satellite networks is the combination of IP and optical switching to achieve high end-to-end throughput by exploiting a mesh network of free space optical links (c.f. Section 4.4.5). In this case, SATs could be used to identify different optical network segments.

4.4.4 Traffic engineering and service management

There are several techniques for achieving packet-level traffic engineering in the network layer [10]. Traffic engineering is the process of selecting end-to-end paths by considering link attributes to satisfy a set of traffic constraints. To achieve low delays, routing may be performed in advance of sending traffic (e.g., by using *path computation element* [11]), in which case some form of encapsulation, as provided by semantic routing, is needed to bind the traffic to the selected route(s). In this chapter, we look at load balancing and its impact on a service-centric architecture. In a service-centric network, load balancing is crucial to improve the distribution of service requests and corresponding traffic load in the network. Since processing service requests is a time-consuming process, a suitable balancing of load among service providers can improve the overall performance of the system, namely in terms of service latency. Moreover, defining services as chains of network functions is important for the overall system performance, namely when the execution of different functions is interdependent, as is the case of a video-encoding service, where the video needs to be fetched before being encoded. Leveraging an ICN framework to support services raises challenges, especially in the scope of service management in general and load balancing. Managing services instead of data objects is different in the sense that service results are not readily available but needs to be prepared upon request, which does not happen with the typical get-data request in ICN. Moreover, the cost of a service request has an impact not only on the used bandwidth, but also on CPU time, memory usage, and storage IO. This has an implication in the adaptation of an ICN platform to provide services. For instance, the NDN broadcast-forwarding strategy is extremely expensive, since every Interest (i.e., request in NDN) is forwarded to all possible faces, it will reach all service replicas, each of which will execute the service request, but only one response reaches the consumer. In this case, the network should make sure that a service Interest reaches only one replica, preferably the least busy one in order to serve clients as fast as possible. In other words, load balancing is essential to distribute the load among service replicas in NDN. In NDN, a forwarding strategy is responsible for choosing the best face to forward an Interest, based on information provided stored in the *forwarding information base (FIB)*, and/or some measurements such as link load (e.g., via DLEP [27]). Choosing the best face in the FIB can reduce response time and distribute the load over service replicas. Several forwarding strategies are proposed in NDN, based on local information, or on network probing. The latter relies mainly on *round trip time (RTT)* which comes with some challenges: RTT may not capture the state of the service provider; mixing RTTs of service requests and data requests can lead to a large variance. While strategies based on local information led to lower overhead in the network, they also may be less efficient than probing methods in capturing different metrics from the network. While conventional load-balancing algorithms, such as round robin [29] and heuristic load balancing [19], are highly related to balance traffic load in NDN, raises some challenges in what concerns the selection of the best metrics, from RTT to server metrics, and queue sizes. Another challenge is related to the location of the load-balancing functionality: distributed in routers or implemented in a controller. In the former case, load balancing is implemented by forwarding strategies. This method does not have a single point of failure, but it can be demanding in terms of resources. Solutions based on a controller rely on periodic network probing to collect information about link utilization and switch/router load. Such information can be used by a reinforcement-learning agent to adapt the link weights aiming to balance the load in queues, or to compute new optimal paths upon congestion, being the forwarding process implemented in P4.

4.4.5 Hybrid optical and IP networking

Satellite networks able to handle large traffic volumes require suitable methods to combine the high-throughput capabilities of FSO links with a more intelligent forwarding of packets to react to dynamic network conditions in a useful amount of time. Hence, it is important to investigate efficient methods to converge the optical transport on layer 1 with the routing functionality on layer 3. Over the past ten years, there have been tremendous advancements in *dense wavelength division multiplexing (DWDM)* optics and routing technologies toward more efficient cards. In this context, it makes sense to move the DWDM transponder into the router by simplifying the DWDM system and leveraging routing technology to replace its functionality. The optical and routing convergence was made possible by the development of a set of technology, such as small DWDM optics and programmable network protocol stacks (c.f. Section 4.4.2). The benefits of such a hybrid optical/routing system include less space and power consumption, which are essential in satellite systems. However, the usage of point-to-point DWDM line systems is typically not practical for complex networks, as is the case of large-scale satellite networks based on FSO links and varying levels of traffic demands. Hence, such network could be deployed based on a *reconfigurable optical add-drop multiplexer (ROADM)*, allowing wavelengths to be added and dropped by networked nodes, allowing them to optically pass through a site in a multi-site topology. However, ROADM devices are expensive. Hence, a solution may pass by replacing the ROADM architecture by levering high-capacity DWDM links with semantic routing (c.f. Section 4.4.3) along with a programmable data plane. This means that where before traffic would optically pass through a router, it is now switched. In this scenario rather than using optical path protection, semantic routing based on segmented routing topology independent loop-free alternate will be used to perform path redundancy over segmented routed paths used to connect service instances. The assumption is that by combining high-capacity ZR+ DWDM optics with relatively inexpensive routers powered by semantic routing, traffic paths can be managed within the router. This means that instead of creating optical end-to-end circuits that may break with high probability in a dynamic large-scale satellite network, semantic routing-based traffic engineering should be used to create end-to-end services. Since traffic does not cross a network optically, routers must process every packet that traverses it. This is a concern in terms of latency when we consider traditional software-based routers. However, today's modern ASIC-based routers equate to a Layer 3 switch that can switch packets within 4–6 microseconds. This time includes the serialization delay of the packet, which decreases as link speeds increase. An example is the Xilinx Versal product, based on the adaptable computing acceleration platform (ACAP), which is a hybrid acceleration platform that combines the programmability of CPUs, the performance of ASICs, and adaptability of FPGAs. Still, in what concerns delays, the IP layer would have to re-converge if the primary link was lost. With topology-independent loop-free alternate (TILFA), as used in segment routing, it is possible to achieve ¡50 millisecond fail-over times, since alternative paths are identified in advance, and packets can be rerouted almost instantaneously.

4.5 Cognitive Service-centric Networking

In the next 10 years, it is assumed that future large-scale satellite networks will evolve to become a global digital infrastructure, able of hosting many services with diverse, and in many cases, extreme requirements. In this scenario, it is assumed that network management systems based on partially automated operations will not be efficient. For such complex cases, it requires the investigation of cognitive networks: networking technologies able to acquire knowledge, by learning or reasoning. In this process, the network needs to be able to sense the surrounding context, for instance, to be capable of finding patterns in resource usage and taking actions to optimize this usage. A cognitive network may achieve a higher level of automation able to replace or complement most of nowadays network management and configuration tasks. Initially, the human operator will guide the network in learning and taking decisions, but eventually, the network may start operating in a full autonomous manner, in which case the network operator is merely supervising and managing the automated operation but is no longer actively taking part in configuration tasks, as the system itself can continuously optimize its performance towards set of operation intents. In order for the network to be autonomous, its management system needs to have the needed level of freedom to take decisions. One way to support this is via the deployment of orchestration systems that aim to control the network via intents. An intent can be seen as a formal specification of all expectations including requirements, goals, and constraints given to a networking system. Intents specify what goal to achieve, contrary to many control interfaces today, where the system is rather instructed what to do and how to do it.

In large-scale satellite networks, orchestration scalability may require a distributed intelligence approach for decision-making. For instance, services with real-time requirements lead to the need to place decision-making agents close to the functions they control. Cognitive networks may be defined in a hierarchical manner rooted in an orchestrator able to handle top-level intents sent by humans via a specific interface. For the cognitive network to scale, the orchestrator will coordinate a set of multiple intent managers (c.f. Figure 4.3) distributed across the network.

Each intent manager is responsible for a specific part of the network, which can include a specific infrastructure of a list of others' intent managers. Each intent manager implements a set of cognitive functions that enable it to observe the network under its control, draw conclusions from the acquired data, evaluate alternatives, and take action to fulfill the intents. Each cognitive function can use artificial intelligence features to draw conclusions from acquired data and available knowledge. Examples of such features include machine-learning models that can produce insights and machine-reasoning

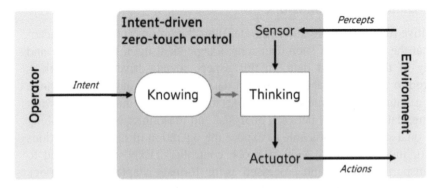

Figure 4.3   High-level perspective of an intent manager.

capabilities to reason around insights. This means that each cognitive function is able to implement a control loop for a specific service and resource set, consisting of four functional blocks: (1) monitor the environment under control; (2) analyze and learn from data; (3) based on the analysis, reasoning about what to do; and (4) based on the reasoning take action to fulfill the intent. The decision can be passed to the correspondent intent manager, which will perform the needed coordination action between the action taken by different cognitive functions in order to fulfill a set of higher-level intent that encompasses all the fine-grain intents passed to each cognitive function. Since different intent managers can act on the same services in other different parts of the network, there is the need to automatically resolve any resulting conflicts. Such a control loop requires the implementation of a data-driven framework able to provide cognitive functions with reliable and useful data in a timely and secure manner in order to support the four functional blocks mentioned above. Since the learning and reasoning process used by cognitive functions can have outputs that are unexpected or seemingly unpredictable, the cognitive network needs to be based on implementation of a trustworthy artificial intelligence system. Finally, actions taken as a result of a reasoning process need to be verified against a set of intents added to the system during runtime. This means that there is a need to perform conflict detection and resolution between the actions taken over the same services in different parts of the network, which are controlled by different intent managers.

The next sub-section further analyzes the identified building blocks: data-driven framework; trustful artificial intelligence; and intent-based automation.

4.5.1 Data-driven framework

Cognitive functions make automatic decisions based on facts or data, meaning that the accuracy of such decisions is dependent upon the quantity and quality of the collected data. In this aspect, a data-driven framework is required to provide reliable and useful data in a timely and secure manner. Such a data-driven framework has a set of core components for network probing, data exchange, network analysis, and reasoning. Network probing relies on a set of methods able to expose the operation of network functions via, for instance, virtual taps or probe controllers. Exposed data need to be transported, stored, and processed, using formats adapted to the service required by the consumer of the data pipeline. The processed data are used to create insights about the operation of the network allowing the real-time adaptation of end-to-end service. The data pipeline used by the data-driven operation framework can be described as a network service, in which case it can be handled by the service-centric networking approach described in Section 4.4.1. The learning process used by the data-driven framework is supported by machine-learning modules that contain models that need to be trained. For model training and model execution, different learning modes are possible, such as local, central, federated, transfer, offline, and online learning, depending on the requirements of the machine-learning functionality. The life cycle of models encompasses the preparation, modeling, and validation of datasets, after which models can be deployed and executed. The development of suitable date-driven frameworks encompasses initiatives in different standardization organizations, such as

1. *Open network automation platform (ONAP)* provides a reference architecture for data collection and analytic. ONAP is designed for scalability, being deployed hierarchically, and supporting distributed machine-learning principles like federated learning.
2. Zero-Touch Network and Service Management (ETSI ZSM) specifies an end-to-end architecture based on a framework for multi-domain management that uses specifications from other organizations such as 3GPP.
3. Machine Learning for Future Networks including 5G (ITU-T SG 13 ML5G) proposes a standardized machine-learning pipeline, including model life-cycle management, monitoring model performance, and triggering re-training.

A data-driven framework allows artificial intelligence algorithms to make better decisions, thereby optimizing the management of the network. However, there are several challenges to be tackled such as to understand how new technologies like reinforcement would learning work in a data-driven framework. In the specific case of large-scale satellite networks, it will be important to analyze how to scale the data-driven framework when it is deployed over a large geographic area.

4.5.2 Trustworthy artificial intelligence

A rapid surge in the complexity of artificial intelligence (AI) systems has evolved to such an extent that humans do not understand such systems. This is a challenge when AI-based systems compute outputs that are unexpected or seemingly unpredictable. Hence, to be trusted by humans, a cognitive network needs to be based on trustworthy AI methods such as predictions, decisions, and recommendations, according to the European Commission's ethical guidelines for trustworthy AI. AI methods are generally categorized into machine learning, machine reasoning, and the interplay of both. The interplay between learning and reasoning can be understood from ETSI ZSM autonomic loops architecture, where data collected from the environment are analyzed using machine-learning approaches, and the derived information and insights are fed to machine reasoning systems to compute decisions. In this process, involving machine learning and reasoning, it is important to incorporate trust at different levels. An approach can pass by including explainability for data and applying explainability to both machine learning and reasoning as well as to the interplay between them by feeding the output of a machine-learning model (both its predictions and explanations) into machine reasoning and using the outcome to generate explanations. This proactive placement provides the needed trustworthiness to the AI process, by providing details such as how a model generates predictions, a decision path obtained from a decision tree model, or a rule generated from a simplified model. Based on the scalable hierarchical model of a cognitive network, it is important to understand how to include trustful AI into a scalable system composed of multiple cognitive functions and intent managers. The AI agents of each cognitive function may be autonomous yet be able to achieve consensus among them in order to meet business intents. In such a scenario, it is important for AI agents to generate explanations toward other agents. Consuming explanations from other agents also enables explanations to be tailored to humans by presenting the view from across the full system at a higher level of abstraction. This type of distributed trustful AI is especially crucial for trust in multi-vendor environments where AI agents from various vendors could interact to meet high-level intents, increasing the efficiency of the orchestration and management system.

4.5.3 Intent-based automation

It is envisioned that independently of the level of automation of the cognitive network, its control will be done by the network operator through high-level operational goals in the form of intents. An intent in an autonomous system is ideally expressed in a declarative fashion, that is, as a utility-level goal that describes the properties of a satisfactory outcome rather than prescribing a specific solution. This gives the system flexibility to explore various solution options and find the optimal one. Unlike traditional software systems, where requirements are analyzed offline to detect and resolve conflicts prior to implementation, intents are added to an autonomous system during runtime. Adaptation to changed intent as well as conflict detection and resolution are, therefore, essential capabilities of an autonomous system. One essential type of intent is related to the specification of services. Service-specific intents state expected functional and performance characteristics. *Service level agreements (SLAs), service level specifications (SLSs), service level objectives (SLOs),* and *topology and orchestration specification for cloud applications (TOSCA)* models are all examples of service-specific intents that are used on different levels in the operations' stack. An autonomous system requires intents to be formally defined in a machine-readable way, but the broad range of considerations involved, and their abstract semantics are often difficult to structure. Techniques from knowledge management and semantic modeling should enable the creation of an ontology of intents, following an extensible model based for instance on the *resource description framework (RDF)* standards.

4.6 Conclusions

Following the 6G vision, a large-scale satellite network is destined to realize full coverage for an *Internet of Everything*. To cope with complex and changing scenarios, a (multi-orbit) large-scale satellite network must implement a flexible and highly efficient architecture. As Internet is more and more oriented to services, only a service-oriented architecture can insure a seamless integration of satellite networks and the Internet. Hence, this chapter starts by identifying a set of design choices for a service-centric network architecture for large-scale satellite networks. Services are described as chains of network functions that are capable of real-time perception and AI reasoning. Since ICN is foreseen as a prominent candidate to replace the current host-centric Internet architecture, this chapter explains how to extend it to support a network operation based on services. One such extension is the definition of a programmable data plane to support the time-variant services. Furthermore, the flexible-forwarding strategies implemented in such programmable data plane need to be combined with routing strategies able to consider different service semantics. An applicability case for such semantic control plan is the combination of IP and optical switching to achieve high end-to-end throughput by exploiting a mesh network of free-space optical links. An increased level of autonomy of such complex satellite network can be achieved by the usage of cognitive methods for sensing, learning, and reasoning, allowing the network to grow in scale and diversity of services, and the operator to focus on more strategic challenges. Such cognitive network is expected to be fully controlled by intent-based technologies, simplifying the task for humans to define services and operational goals. Overall, this chapter aims to help in redesigning the architecture of future large-scale satellite networks aiming to achieve a powerful, flexible, and intelligent networking experience, while seamlessly integrated into the terrestrial networking infrastructure. This is done based on a novel cognitive service-centric networking architecture.

References

[1] David Barach, Leonardo Linguaglossa, Damjan Marion, Pierre Pfister, Salvatore Pontarelli, and Dario Rossi. High-speed software data plane via vectorized packet processing. IEEE Communications Magazine, (12), 2018.

[2] B. E. Carpenter, S. Jiang, and G. Li. Service oriented internet protocol. Technical report, IETF, 5 2020. draft-jiang-service-oriented-ip-03.

[3] S. Choi, X. Long, M. Shahbaz, S. Booth, A. Keep, J. Marshall, and C. Kim. Pvpp: A programmable vector packet processor. ACM Symposium on SDN Research, pages 197–198, 2017.

[4] Cisco. Vni global fixed and mobile internet traffic forecasts," cisco,. Technical report, Cisco, 2019.

[5] T. Dasu, Y. Kanza, and D. Srivastava. Packets for location-aware software-defined networking in the presence of virtual network functions. In ACM International Conference on Advances in Geographic Information Systems, Redondo Beach, California, USA, 2017.

[6] Seweryn Dynerowicz and Paulo Mendes. Named-data networking in opportunistic networks. In ACM Information Centric Networking conference, Berlin, Germany, 9 2017.

[7] G. Xylomenos et al. A survey of information-centric networking research. IEEE Communications Surveys and Tutorials, 16(2):1024–1049, 2014.

[8] S. Srinivasan et al. Ccnxserv: Dynamic service scalability in information-centric networks. In IEEE International Conference on Communications, Ottawa, Canada, 6 2012.

[9] Tarik Taleb et al. Whitepaper on 6g networking. Technical Report 6, The 6G Flagship consortium, 6 2020.

[10] AA. Farrel. Overview and principles of internet traffic engineering. Technical report, IETF, 8 2021. Request for Comments: 3272bis.

[11] A. Farrel, J.-P. Vasseur, and J. Ash. A path computation element (pce)-based architecture. Technical report, IETF, 8 2006. Request for Comments: 4655.

[12] Juan Fraire, Olivier De Jonckere, and Scott Burleigh. Routing in the space internet: A contact graph routing tutoria. jan 2021.

[13] M. Giordani and M. Zorzi. Non-terrestrial networks in the 6g era: Challenges and opportunities. mar 2021.

[14] D. Grossman. New terminology and clarifications for diffserv. Technical report, IETF, 4 2002. Request for Comments: 3260.

[15] J. Halpern and C. Pignataro. Service function chaining (sfc) architecture. Technical report, IETF, 10 2015. Request for Comments: 7665.

[16] Mark Handley. Delay is not an option: Low latency routing in space. In ACM Hotnets, nov 2018.

[17] Focust Group on Network 2030 ITU-T. New services and capabilities for network 2030: Description, technical gap and performance target analysis. Technical report, ITU-T, oct 2019.

[18] S. Burleigh K. Scott. Bundle protocol specification. Technical report, IETF, nov 2007.

[19] A. Kaur and B. Kaur. Load balancing in tasks using honey bee behavior algorithm in cloud computing. In IEEE international conference on wireless networks and embedded systems, Graz, Austria, 10 2016.

[20] M. Krol and I. Psaras. Nfaas: Named function as a service. In t' ACM Conference on Information-Centric Networking, Berlin, Germany, 9 2017.

[21] S. Luo Z. Ye X. Du M. Guizani L. Luo, H. Yu. Scalable explicit path control in softwaredefined networks. 2019.

[22] D. Mansour, T. Braun, and C. Anastasiades. Nextserve framework: Supporting services over content-centric networking. In IFIP International

Conference on Wired Wireless Internet Communications, Paris, France, 5 2014.

[23] Paulo Mendes, Rute C Sofia, Vassilis Tsaoussidis, Sotiris Diamantopoulos, and Joset' Soares. Information-centric routing for opportunistic wireless networks. 2018.

[24] Waldir Moreira and Paulo Mendes. Survey on opportunistic routing for delay/disruption tolerant networks. Technical report, COPELABS, 11 2010. Technical Report SITI-TR11-02.

[25] Waldir Moreira, Paulo Mendes, and Susana Sargento. Assessment model for opportunistic routing. In IEEE Latincom, Belem, Brazil, 10 2011.

[26] P. Quinn, U. Elzur, and C. Pignataro. Network service header (nsh). Technical report, IETF, 1 2018. Request for Comments: 8300.

[27] S. Ratliff, S. Jury, D. Satterwhite, and R. Taylor. Dynamic link exchange protocol (dlep). Technical report, IETF, 6 2017. Request for Comments: 8175.

[28] P. Ren, X. Wang, B. Zhao, C. Wu, and H. Sun. Opensrn: A software-defined semantic routing network architecture. In IEEE Conference on Computer Communications Workshops, Hong Kong, China, 2015.

[29] X. Ren, R. Lin, and H. Zou. A dynamic load balancing strategy for cloud computing platform based on exponential smoothing forecast. In IEEE international conference on cloud computing and intelligence systems, Beijing, China, 9 2011.

[30] Christos-Alexandros Sarros, Sotiris Diamantopoulos, Sergi Rene, Ioannis Psaras, Adisorn Lertsinsrubtavee, Carlos Molina-Jimenez, Paulo Mendes, Rute Sofia, Arjuna Sathiaseelan, George Pavlou, Jon Crowcroft, and Vassilis Tsaoussidis. Connecting the edges: A universal, mobile-centric, and opportunistic communications architecture. Comm. Mag., 56(2):136–143, Feb 2018.

[31] Vasilios Siris, Christopher Ververidis, George Polyzos, and Konstantinos Liolis. Information-centric networking (icn) architectures for integration of satellites into the future internet. In IEEE ESTEL, oct 2012.

[32] J. Strassner, Sung-Su K., and J. Won-Ki. Semantic routing for improved network management in the future internet. Book Chapter Springer, Recent Trends in Wireless and Mobile Networks, 2010.

[33] C. Tschudin and M. Sifalakis. Named functions and cached computations. In IEEE Consumer Communications and Networking Conference, Las Vegas, USA, 1 2014.

[34] A. Hooke L. Torgerson R. Durst K. Scott K. Fall H. Weiss V. Cerf, S. Burleigh. Delaytolerant networking architecture. Technical report, IETF, apr 2007.

[35] Koji Yamazaki, Yoshihiro Nakajima, Takahiro Hatano, Hirokazu Takahashi, Akihiko Miyazaki, and Katsuhiro Shimano. Innovating a reprogrammable network with sdnet. Xcell Software Journal, page 24, 12 2015.

[36] B. Zaluski, B. Rajtar, H. Habjani, M. Baranek, N. Slibar, R. Petracic, and T. Sukser. Terastream implementation of all ip new architecture. In International Convention on Information and Communication Technology, Electronics and Microelectronics, 2013.

[37] Lixia Zhang, Alexander Afanasyev, Jeffrey Burke, Van Jacobson, kc claffy, Patrick Crowley, Christos Papadopoulos, Lan Wang, and Beichuan Zhang. Named data networking. Technical report, NDN Project Consortium, 2019.

5

The Role of Socially Aware Networking in Supporting 6G IoT

Rute C. Sofia

Rute C. Sofia, fortiss research institute for software intensive services and systems, Germany,
E-mail: sofia@fortiss.org

Abstract

Large-scale IoT environments have been growing fast via the advancement of 5G, 6G, advanced wireless standards, associated with advancements in multiple other technological fields. These environments, which are composed by a wide variety of cyber-physical systems, including sensors, actuators, mobile personal smartphones, have the capability to further assist societal development and societal needs across different sectors, for example, education, health, and economy.

In future 6G IoT deployments, a high number of mobile devices shall be exchanging data across heterogeneous wireless environments, in a way that mimics up to some extent social behavior. Therefore, services shall be further decentralized and local, as occurs already in different sectors, for example, energy. There is, therefore, a natural need and a tendency to integrate social awareness into the networking layers and to push computation and networking operations as close as possible to the end-user, to the so-called "far edge."

This chapter discusses the status of IoT, and trends that are starting to occur, such as edge computing decentralization and integration of artificial intelligence on the edge, to then propose a few directions to be tackled, advocating the need to integrate context awareness into the network, based on an interdisciplinary approach that should bring principles of social awareness to the network, derived from an interdisciplinary group dynamics design approach, combining networking, and social sciences.

Keywords: Edge, IoT, Social Awareness, Machine Learning.

5.1 Introduction

With the deployment of *Internet of Things (IoT)* across different vertical domains, for example, manufacturing, smart cities, agriculture, the Internet has reached a new era in its evolutionary track where its further development shall relate on its power as a complex social platform. New types of social networking keep on emerging: *augmented reality (AR)* and *virtual reality (AR)* are gaining continuous ground across different vertical domains; and wireless networking continues evolving, supporting further *device-to-device (D2D)* communication across different environments. In the context of 6G, the *massive machine type communications (mMTC)* paradigm [1] integrates the notion of large, dense deployments of IoT (interconnected) "Things" which may directly communicate with minor or even without human intervention. This higher degree of autonomy is expected to be the basis for the development of next-generation densely deployed IoT/sensing services, which in this chapter shall be referred to as *6G IoT* services. Enabling 6G IoT is today being envisioned by adapting the networking layers to support low-power communications while supporting challenges such as mobility, real-time high-definition applications, etc.

However, a central aspect to 6G IoT is the fact that massive deployments of IoT devices will have to take into consideration a high number of mobile personal devices, or devices that are carried and controlled by end-users. For instance, smart glasses or smartphones are examples of such devices. Personal mobile devices today already integrate a wide variety of sensing tools that can, among others, capture different aspects of the individual roaming routines and social behavior by relying on the user's input (*participatory sensing*) or by relying on non-intrusive sensing (*opportunistic sensing*) [2].

As technology becomes more pervasive, these devices that are carried and surround people are collecting data that can be used to better support daily activities across different vertical domains, giving rise to a wide variety of *Mobile Crowd Sensing (MCS)* applications [3]. For instance, today there are several tools that bring awareness to our fitness routine, or even to our daily activity patterns, for example, by performing individual activity recognition and pattern inference. Individual sleep patterns, motion, as well

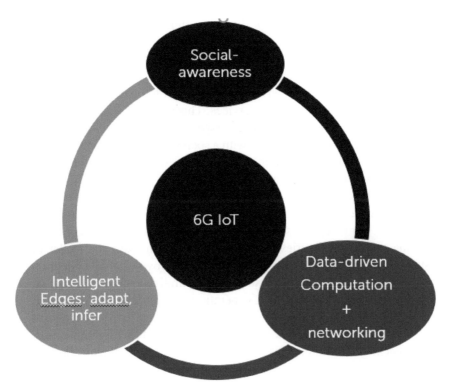

Figure 5.1 6G IoT vision: data-network-compute pillars to achieve an Edge-Cloud adaptive continuum.

as other activity and behavioral patterns are aspects that can be tracked and inferred via current personal devices [4, 5],. There are also several pervasive computing frameworks that attempt to gather healthcare data across edge–cloud in a way to assist in a better prevention of diseases, or to improve the lifecycle crop aspects, or improve energy distribution across micro-grids, for instance. Therefore, MCS, which is expected to require some level of collective autonomous behavior, will be a key category of applications within 6G IoT.

Creating an autonomous collective and sustainable behavior requires specific aspects to be worked, as illustrated in Figure 5.1. First, it is important to jointly address, in the context of edge computing for IoT, computational and networking functions that can support, by design, aspects such as security/trustworthiness, mobility support, decentralized, and flexible naming spaces. This is further discussed in Section 5.3. Second, edge functions require the integration of behavior learning and inference, that is, ML adaptation to decentralized edges as shall be debated in Section 5.4. Third, the networking infrastructure needs to become more flexible, intent, and context driven. Social awareness needs to be integrated into the networking layers, for communication and network management to be handled in a way that can truly support people-centric services. This requires addressing social awareness both from a computer science perspective (e.g., physical proximity based on signal, time, space), together with a social psychology approach that defines social proximity aspects, for example, derived from social interaction modeling, aspects which are debated in Section 5.5.

The aim of this chapter is, therefore, to provide a debate on interdisciplinary social-aware aspects that need to be addressed in networking to better support 6G IoT. For that purpose, after this section, Section 5.2 covers related work, citing relevant categories of prior work that can assist the reader in understanding the concepts discussed. Section 5.3 provides an overview on the status of IoT, the trend toward service decentralization, and the role of edge computing in this context. Next-generation IoT services are expected to thrive and to be a key set of 6G services to be supported by MCS one such service. Section 5.4 addresses the current challenges to bring intelligence to the Edge in next-generation IoT, as such integration is key to allowing 6G IoT deployments to operate in a collectively intelligent way. Section 5.5 covers principles of social-aware networking, relevant to 6G IoT, explaining how social awareness is today being applied and what are the challenges. Section 5.6 provides recommendations for the integration of an interdisciplinary approach to social awareness in the networking layers, while Section 5.7 concludes the chapter.

5.2 Related Work

Within the context of pervasive computing, several efforts have been developed to integrate context awareness into computing, derived from an interdisciplinary approach between computer science and social sciences. The aim of this effort is to embed some form of intelligence and self-awareness into computational systems, to benefit societal needs. This is the case of the *Relevance and Cognition for Self-Awareness in a Content-centric Internet (RECOGNITION)* [6], which aimed to develop a radical new approach for embedding self-awareness in ICT systems. The RECOGNITION project was based on the processes underlying human self-awareness, exploiting the fact that humans are the fundamental basis for high-performance autonomic processes.

A second relevant category of work, *social sensing*, has been focusing on inferring the structure of social ties based on personal-scale information, such as sleep patterns and its relation to a mood [7]. However, it is also feasible to consider the emotional correlation between different users of the same cluster, even without the need to have social ties. If one finds such a correlation then self-organizing models can evolve beyond influence, selection, or contextual modeling, and closer to the way humans organize interaction. Rachuri et al., for instance, have been delving into work concerning mobile technology to assist in social psychological research [3, 8]. Burns et al. have developed work focused on the usage of mobile devices to recognize individual activity patterns and link them to specific emotional states, or to early indicators of potential issues [9].

A third category of work has been focusing on *online social networks (OSNs)* in regard to a better understanding of social virtual ties (e.g., how content is shared, and how new friendships are built) [10]. This line of work is relevant in the context of understanding social networking dynamics aspects such as reinforcement, popularity, centrality. Nevertheless, OSN work is focused on weak ties which do not necessarily represent real-time interconnections between users.

The need to consider sociability aspects in the context of the use of large-scale sensing applications, of which MCS is an example, addressed sociability aspects mostly based on geo-location similarity derived from affinity networks built based on calls, wireless network visits, for instance [11, 12]. In this context, several context recognition frameworks and tools have addressed the capability of personal devices to sense and recognize the context of a user [13–15].

More recently, due to the COVID-19 pandemic, and in association with the development of lighter ML tools, related work has been focused on the use of edge-enabled frameworks to assist a more relevant collection of data [16], and therefore to be able to provide a close-to-real-time inference of epidemiological spreading [17].

In the context of beyond 5G services and 6G services, several efforts are addressing the need to integrate social awareness into different computational realms. For instance, Zhang et al. address social-aware caching in vehicular networks, proposing a deep learning-based caching scheme that is based on an interdisciplinary approach that takes into consideration cache usage, cache cloud formation, and social awareness [18]. Li et al. propose a context and social aware approach for online beam selection within the context of mmWave vehicular communications [19], where the social information relates with a probabilistic encounter approach based on a mix of user preferences and vehicle preferences. Social awareness and mobility similarity have been explored by Zhang et al. in the context of video delivery in 5G ultra-dense networks, resulting in lower packet loss, lower cache utilization, and lower control overhead [20].

Summarizing the application of context-awareness and of social awareness is a recognized need within the context of dense IoT deployments. Still, this integration has so far been developed mostly derived from a limited interdisciplinary perspective. Within this problem space, this chapter aims at bringing awareness to the challenges expected in next-generation IoT environments, such as 6G IoT environments, and how context awareness and in particular some level of social awareness can be integrated and why.

5.3 The Need for Joint Computation and Data-driven Networking

The generic IoT definition [21] concerns "a global infrastructure for the information society, enabling services by interconnecting (physical and virtual) things based on existing and evolving interoperable information and communication technologies." Nevertheless, today IoT still concerns the network of everyday objects that can collect and transmit data via the internet. One of the major limitations to the evolution of the IoT concept is the fact that the transmission over IoT is not trivial due on the one hand to the heterogeneity of hardware and software involved, and on the other hand, due to the networking nature of Internet, which relies on principles of "host reachability" and not principles of "data reachability." Hence, the natural evolution of IoT requires an adequate interconnection of three different aspects: (i) intelligent cyber-physical systems; (ii) contextualization derived from data analytics and predictive analysis; and (iii) smart connectivity. By smart connectivity, it is meant that the notion of connectivity does not imply that devices need to be always connected to the internet. For instance, specific sets of devices can connect opportunistically, derived from local connectivity opportunities, not necessarily implying internet connectivity.

A notion of social aware and data-driven communications is, therefore, a key aspect missing in IoT. IoT environments are today being supported by varied communication architectures and protocols that embody a host reachability approach instead of a data-driven and data reachability approach.

Future 6G IoT systems need to be designed in a modular, decentralized way. This line of thought has already started. By pushing storage and computation closer to data sources and to consumers of the data, there are several immediate benefits, for example, reduced latency; data locality (more control over one's own data); reduce overall required energy consumption [22]. Still, there is a need to further evolve the design of IoT systems into a smart, context-aware, autonomous design approach.

Our belief is that future 6G IoT systems need to integrate an interdisciplinary design approach that better intertwines computational and the networking perspective, i.e., to consider principles from current softwarization and data-driven paradigms (in-network computing) [23, 24], such as ICN, SDN, to support the development of a socially aware infrastructure for IoT. By doing so, it will be feasible to better address challenges such as data source/consumer and networking device mobility; end-to-end data privacy; better support of caching and processing of larger volumes of data; allowing a faster and more reliable interconnection of more consumers and producers of data, in an interoperable way.

In this future design, the role of *decentralized edge computing* [25] becomes preponderant, as IoT services are becoming increasingly decentralized and communications need to address better the Publish/Subscribe principle, taking into consideration the need to support simultaneous data exchange between multiple sources and multiple destinations. Edge/fog computing [26, 27] envisions a smooth migration of applications and services between different physical and virtual machines to best meet the application requirements. In practice, such migration still requires a high degree of human intervention, as can be observed in the ETSI *mobile edge computing (MEC)* architecture [28], where supported scenarios consider migration mostly for the purpose of backup and restore of applications, or for redundancy.

5.3.1 Challenges to be addressed

There are, however, some immediate challenges. First and foremost is the need to support mobility, and sovereignty aspects. It is also required to consider that "edge" is an elastic concept that is not tied to a specific infrastructure boundary, and therefore, such edge is also reaching end-user devices, such as smartphones, or smart sensors placed in industrial shop-floor environments, as well as satellite constellations. The next step relates to making IoT systems flexible and autonomous. Flexibility shall stem both from the capability to abstract the components and interconnect them based on a semantic design approach. The semantic composition needs also to be addressed from a joint computational and network perspective [29].

5.4 Moving Toward Autonomous Decentralized Edges

Intelligence at the edge, also known as *edge AI* [30, 31] is focused on bringing capabilities to edge devices so that IoT autonomous systems can sense, learn, and react to their surroundings in a way that can best support the IoT services being carried out. Edge AI allows the development of local processes to handle higher-level decisions close to data sources. It also creates the possibility for systems to behave autonomously, from an individual and collective perspective.

Edge AI as a field of research in the context of IoT has as main goal to support the following aspects: behavior automation; context awareness; adaptation. By *automation* here, it is meant to reduce the need for manual intervention. *Context awareness* relates to meeting the specific needs of applications, infrastructure, and of end-user. *Adaptation* refers to the system learning and adapting capabilities, to best meet overall requirements that may change over time and space.

The captured data can be stored in a decentralized way across different edges and sent to the cloud for specific processing derived from behavioral learning and inference. Pre-training and learning are traditionally part of a continuous process, so that edge devices can learn in close to real time, while they process captured information. This corresponds to the traditional architectural model that supports intelligence (i.e., AI training and classification) across edge–cloud environments.

The increasing service decentralization being observed in IoT and described in Section 5.3 requires, however, additional support for the adequate integration of intelligence on the edge, thus, giving rise to true autonomous and adaptable systems.

The first challenge in this context relates to having to handle high data volumes. The increasing number of data sources in different environments during 2021 already reached over 10 billion active IoT devices being an estimation for 2030 over 25.4 billion devices, and the amount of data generated by IoT devices is expected to reach 73.1 ZB (zettabytes) by 2025[1].

---

[1] https://dataprot.net/statistics/iot-statistics/. Consulted on 30.11.2021.

A second challenge relates to the type of data and interoperability. The increasing number of active IoT devices provides the ability to leverage new types of data, referred to as "smart data" or "small data" [32], resulting from tracking various aspects of citizens' routines, for example, roaming habits, application usage, and location preferences. Small data bring in a new level of granularity in terms of features and correspond also to lower volumes of data than "big data," introducing new problems in terms of data validation and processing [33]. A third challenge relates to the ML engineering adaptation to edge environments. ML algorithms have been developed for cloud-based environments. Such algorithms (e.g., federated learning approaches) can be easily replicated in the so-called *"near edge"* infrastructure (rf. to Figure 5.2) for which a reference architecture is the ETSI MEC, where powerful computational devices are placed on an area still under the reach of the operator but closer to data sources, thus, often simply replicating, at a lesser extent and for a specific local purpose, the cloud computational environment. However, the current decentralization trend in IoT services and large-scale deployments requires addressing the integration of AI and ML on *"far edge"* scenarios, where the "far edge" corresponds to the infrastructure deployed within customer premises, closer to data sources, for example, a shop floor, a shopping mall, a stadium, home [25].

Of relevancy for 6G, IoT applications are the possibility to run ML in embedded devices, i.e., TinyML [34, 35]. A trend of research focused on this problem is to rely embedded AI applications running in smartphones that are to export the finished model (graph) after training. For instance, a *deep learning* (DL) model is prototyped in a DL framework such as Caffe or TensorFlow but trained on the cloud or on a powerful edge controller, often integrating several GPUs. The finished model can then be exported to the far-edge personal device. However, it should be highlighted that smartphones are today powerful computational devices, with storage and computational capability, being their main constrain on battery consumption. While common IoT devices are even more constrained in terms of storage, memory, computational power, and energy dissipation.

5.4.1 Challenges to be addressed

Bringing intelligence to the far edge requires devising decentralized edge-computing architectures, going beyond the MEC architecture, integrating scenarios with frequent mobility, and decentralized trust mechanisms. Challenges to address comprise, among other aspects i) how to support AI

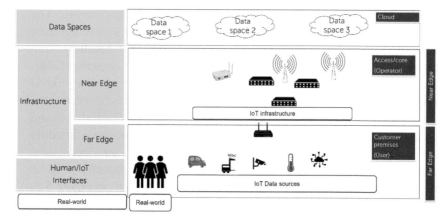

Figure 5.2   IoT end-to-end representation with the far-, near-edge, and cloud environments.

engineering on such decentralized scenarios, via distributed AI approaches; ii) which methods best serve the challenges and constrains posed by realistic far-edge scenarios, in particular in regard to Industrial IoT scenarios; iii) how can ML models be adapted (TinyML) to serve the constrains of IoT sensors (embedded devices), supporting challenges such as intermittent connectivity, mobility management.

Regarding the operationalization of AI on decentralized edge scenarios, distributed AI methods, such as federated learning, are starting points for the support of intelligence in the edge. The use of distributed AI methods needs, nonetheless, to consider new challenges such as constrains of different devices, not forgetting personal smart devices (such as smartphones, which are today the basis for MCS services) and yet, at the same time, considering new edges, such as envisioning smart satellite constellations as potential edges. Furthermore, such discussion must not only consider individual devices as basis, but also how to best provide the underlying networking architecture to best support distributed model training and eventually classification.

Intelligent edge solutions must also be able to handle higher levels of automation, mobility in terms of both physical and virtual machines, and data sources (traffic and data localization). In addition, future applications will also need to consider that containerized applications run across edge and cloud in a way that is not necessarily bound by network policies or geographic boundaries. Edge nodes are therefore expected to have a higher degree of embodied individual and collective intelligence and automation.

A few additional challenges in this context are i) up to which point can ML decentralization be reached; ii) which methods best serve the challenges and constrains posed by realistic far edge scenarios, about Industrial IoT scenarios; iii) how can ML models be adapted to serve the constrains of IoT sensors (embedded devices), supporting challenges as well such as intermittent connectivity; mobility management.

5.5 Social-aware Networking for IoT

Social-aware context has already been applied up to some extent in opportunistic wireless routing [36, 37]. It has also been extensively applied in social mobility modeling [38–40]. Prior attempts to integrate social-aware context have been somewhat limited due to the lack of computational intelligence of the involved devices. For instance, several algorithms for self-organizing networks stem from self-organization biological principles [41], or from physical proximity patterns mostly based on a time approach, such as the duration of contacts between devices or based on geo-positioning.

Interaction behavior of devices integrating affinities/similarity of their human carriers or human controllers is relevant to optimize several aspects of 6G IoT. Nevertheless, such improvements require going beyond the integration of physical proximity parameters such as inter-contact times, or relative distance. They require an interdisciplinary approach to the definition of proximity that should stem from the intersection of theories on group dynamics from social science and from computer science. This section introduces specific social-awareness aspects of each field, explaining how they have been applied in the context of networking.

5.5.1 Social-awareness principles from social psychology

Social theories on group formation consider sociological (i.e., behavioral, interactional, institutional, and structural) and psychological (cognitive and representational, motivational, emotional) aspects of social groups. In this context, the term "social network" refers to any set of interconnections between people and there is no definition of a completely closed system. Therefore, the borders of such a network are usually defined based on some specific context where the social network is defined, for example, via an organization, a state, a large-scale social category, or by referring to a personal social network of an individual (i.e., the interconnections between all individuals who are also connected to an individual x) [42]. As also derived from social psychology, groups of interconnected individuals emerge from larger social networks, and this is facilitated by *propinquity*, i.e., the degree proximity that enhances the probability of direct contact [43]. It is also facilitated by spatial proximity and social similarity.

Understanding the different social psychological perspectives on group formation is highly relevant to allow the network to autonomously adapt to the needs of 6G IoT, in the context of dense environments. Relevant aspects to consider are as follows:

1. In dense deployments, the clustering will also be an expression of the general fabric of social networks in a society.
2. Humans generally differentiate in a variety of ways between different people with whom they have social relationships: between in-group members and out-group members, between people with whom they have relations of positive or negative interdependence (or independence), between people with whom they can pursue common goals or not, between people with whom they have closer or more distant relations, and according to what models of relation they use to interact with people. Therefore, aspects such as betweenness, social (roaming) similarity are also relevant to be integrated.
3. When connecting with others, the psychological criteria for establishing and maintaining relations are part of the psychological background as a powerful force that either facilitates or limits people's availability to engage with others. Therefore, establishing modeling of motivation, trust, and reluctancy in engaging is important for better modeling of proximity-based autonomous systems.
4. Reciprocal give-and-take following the model of equality matching can be a basis for group-based networks. However, the need to maintain balance could limit the speed of interactions or contributions to the system.

5.5.2 Social awareness in networking

The Internet and wireless networks are examples of systems that encompass many interconnected devices that have a dynamic presence, due to their mobility and availability. From a human interaction point of view, it is useful to understand the properties of such systems. Community modeling and complex systems have been addressing group dynamics aspects [44, 45].

Six degrees of separation is a theory that advocates that there are specific patterns of interconnection between humans despite the growing demographic density. Attributed to Frigyes Karinthy (1929), this theory has been subject of strong controversy in computer science [46]. Several studies, such as Milgram's small world experiment [47], have been conducted to empirically provide a measurement of connectedness. Despite its controversy, the notion of six degrees of separation is applied in networking and in computer science, to describe networks that are "highly clustered, like regular lattices, yet have small characteristic path lengths, like random graphs" [48]. Several networks exhibit small-world properties, including systems as diverse as the Internet, social groups, and biochemical pathways. Therefore, the perspective that networks form randomly has been shaken by the small-world controversy. It has actually been discovered that the distribution of node degree of several real networks (e.g., Internet and metabolic network) is different from random networks [48]. This is not of an undifferentiated set of nodes, but of distinct clusters (sets of nodes) as well as of distinct *communities*. Detecting communities in a network provides meaningful insights to its structural principles [49]. Therefore, the dynamics of the network over a long period of time may lead to a significant transformation of the network community structure.

Hence, there is a natural need of updating the knowledge about the network structure over time [49].

The study of real social networks, of which the key properties are illustrated in Figure 5.3, led to a good understanding about the interpretation of graphs. During these studies, sociologists approach toward community detection was based on the concept of *hierarchical clustering* [50]. The basic idea is to develop a measure of similarity between pairs of nodes, based on the network structure. Similarity measurement can then be done in several

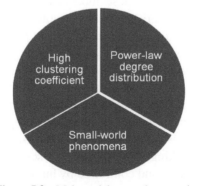

Figure 5.3 Main social network properties.

ways. Sociological studies are mostly focused on the structural equivalence of graphs: two vertices of a graph are said to be structurally equivalent if they have the same set of neighbors, other than each other. However, since the exact structural equivalence is not easy to find in real networks, computer scientists usually define the degree of equivalence on measures such as the Euclidean distance [51], correlation within adjacency matrix [42], and k-components [52]. The application of such measures gave place to several methods for community detection, such as hierarchical clustering, methods based on edge removal and modularity.

5.5.3 Challenges to be addressed

Independently of the applied algorithms, community detection is done based on the connectivity among devices, while a social group is a collection of individuals in spatial and temporal proximity, bound together either by physical boundaries, by social ties, or common goals. This means that current networking models and community detection mechanisms fail in providing information concerning the social meaning and impact of the communication infrastructure.

In this context, social mobility modeling is a relevant field to revisit. In terms of human movement, the works by Barabási et al. Song et al. are highly relevant, as these works debate on the predictable aspects of human movement [53, 54]. More recently a few models emerged, being based on social network theory [40] being one of the first and possibly the most relevant ones due to its inherent social attractiveness (gravitational force) model, the *community mobility model* (CMM) [55]. CMM captures a set of moving nodes, where these nodes form communities based primarily on social relationship among them. These models have evolved to integrate interdisciplinary perspectives derived from a sociological background, as is the case of the *sociological interaction mobility for population simulation (SIMPS)* [56]. Such models are relevant as they allow for a modeling that is closer to real-life scenarios. Social mobility modeling is also relevant in terms of understanding ways to model triggers for human movement; the logic behind individual and collective movement, and up to which point it can be predicted; based on the modeling of such concept, how to quantify specific movement properties. It shows that an interdisciplinary perspective can bring benefits to networking, to heterogeneous scenarios focused on the user, where devices are carried and controlled by humans.

5.6 Interdisciplinary Approach toward Social-aware 6G IoT Networks

IoT devices are evolving beyond the regular role of data source, to become smart devices, with storage, data processing, and networking capabilities. The development of 6G IoT human-centric services require several steps to be taken, and an interdisciplinary approach where integration of social context into the network layers should also be considered.

Integrating social awareness into networking design is increasingly growing and today, due to an extensive effort derived from several initiatives as well as from extensive and wide traces collections, it is globally accepted that there is a relation between social behavior and the user's roaming behavior [34]. It is the social behavior that assists in defining user movement patterns, both from an individual perspective, and from a group perspective. Being capable of learning, in a non-intrusive way, and inferring such behavior and user affinities in a secure way that does not conflict with the private data sphere, will allow 6G IoT environments to truly become human centric. Nevertheless, such integration requires going beyond social awareness based on physical proximity parameters (e.g., time and distance), as debated in Section 5.5. In this section, we debate on the aspects that need to be considered, toward the support of large-scale, 6G environments.

A first step toward the integration of social-aware context into the networking layers requires an interdisciplinary re-definition of networking dynamic properties. An example of a possible approach is provided in Table 5.1, where different networking dynamics properties are described based on their application today, and toward an interdisciplinary, social-aware approach. As described, from an interdisciplinary perspective, key aspects

Table 5.1 (Continued.)

Property	Networking	Interdisciplinary
Degree	Number of incoming and outgoing links a node has. **Individual perspective.**	Number of incoming, outgoing, or reciprocal ties a node has in relation to the total number of ties available in the social network. **Collective perspective.**
Density	Measure of the connectivity level of a network. Density does not always assist in information dissemination.	The proportion of all possible ties that are present in the network being measured. **Density assists in information dissemination.**

Table 5.1   Example of network dynamics properties, and how they can be defined from an interdisciplinary, social-aware perspective.

Reachability	Whether or not nodes are reachable by at least one path. If for 2 specific nodes, there is no available path, then the network is partitioned	Whether or not a node is reachable by another through any set of connections (also considering intermittent connectivity)
Connectivity	Indicates direct connections between nodes.	Whether there is a direct connection from one device to another. Connectivity is another indicator for how information moves through a social structure.
Distance	Measures the relation between two individuals, not necessarily addressing how "close" the two nodes are. **Distance does not provide insight into how long information takes to move through the network.**	Measures how a node is embedded in the social structure by considering node similarity, or cluster similarity metrics. Distance provides insight into how long information takes to move through the network.
Social interaction	Normally provided by inter-contact times or contact frequency/volume. In mobility: social attractiveness is currently being probabilistically modeled.	Measured via physical interaction as well as psychological interaction aspects, for instance: propinquity effect, derived social capital (strength or influence).
Link stability	Derived from the stationary times of two nodes, duration of average inter-contact times, etc.	Common number of neighbors two nodes x and y have over time. A higher common number implies more stability for the link.
Similarity	Derived from the notion of social attraction, for instance, shared interests. Currently addressed probabilistically.	Measured by trust strength, or knowledge increase.
Influence	Inter-contact times and contact duration; cluster density; and betweenness.	Propinquity (probability of social interaction occurring).
Cluster	Set of nodes geographically co-located at a specific instant in time. **Not necessarily sharing similarities.**	Nodes in the same cluster are more similar than in different clusters.
Community	Set of nodes sharing specific interests, **and not necessarily co-located.**	Nodes in the same community are more similar than in different communities.

related to similarity (node and cluster), with the modeling of reciprocity (related to trust), and with the modeling of influence.

Another aspect that is important to address is centrality metrics, which need to be defined from the perspective of social capital. A revision of centrality measures is, therefore, highly relevant in dense 6G IoT deployments, being of relevancy to integrate an interdisciplinary perspective that

Table 5.2 A comparison between centrality measures definitions in networking and derived from social sciences based on social capital definitions.

Property	Networking	Social Sciences
Centrality: determines the relative importance of a vertex within a graph	The impact a node (vertex) has on the graph. Importance here relates to information dissemination.	The influence of the node on the social structure.
Degree centrality: Nodes that have more ties to other nodes have a higher degree of centrality.	Nodes that have more ties to other nodes have a higher degree of centrality. **These are not necessarily better positioned.**	Considers that such nodes are better positioned (influence, information dissemination). Alone, says little about node influence. Together with the degree of centrality of neighbors, provides a better measure.
Betweenness centrality: nodes that have a high probability to occur on a randomly chosen shortest path between two randomly chosen nodes have a high betweenness	Links that are more central assist nodes in better dissemination of information, assuming a plain connectivity model.	Assists in finding "Bridgers": these are nodes that limit clusters (interconnect different clusters).
Closeness centrality: Sum of a node's (shortest-path) distances to any other node y, normalized by the maximum shortest-path length.	A node that has a higher number of shortest-paths than all other nodes has a higher closeness centrality. **It also has a higher probability of becoming a bottleneck.**	High closeness centrality implies better information propagation.
Link Strength: The strength of a tie depends on some measure of interaction between nodes interconnected by that link.	If there is a strong tie between nodes x, y, and another between x and z, nothing can be inferred for a link between x and z.	If there is a strong tie between x, y; and another between y, z; x and z are likely to develop a strong tie as well. This tendency cannot be observed for weak ties.

takes also into consideration a social capital/social interaction perspective to improve dissemination of information, and to take advantage of any possible contact. It is also necessary to revise and to integrate metrics that can measure influence, by integrating social capital metrics. Table 5.2 provides a comparison between current definitions of centrality in networking, and their definition in social sciences, derived from a perspective of social capital. As can be seen, several centrality definitions that may create partitions in the network (bottleneck) are metrics where the same nodes are relevant, from a social capital perspective. The social capital perspective is important for the dissemination of knowledge (knowledge-driven approach), and this will be a key aspect of 6G IoT. Therefore, when applying metrics of the centrality of a node, heuristics should take into consideration additional social properties.

5.7 Conclusions

This chapter provides a debate concerning context-awareness and decentralized edge computing as key aspects to consider within the context of large-scale, people-centric IoT environments, i.e., 6G IoT.

The chapter starts by introducing a perspective on the current IoT development, and the role of decentralized edges for 6G IoT. It then provides an up-to-date perspective on the need to integrate AI on the edge, and existing challenges, advocating as third pillar the need to integrate context awareness into the networking layers, to allow for the development of human-centric networks and consequently, people-centric IoT services. The chapter then provides guidelines on how to achieve human-centric network dynamics, exemplifying with metrics that are today relevant for the development of flexible, autonomous wireless dense environments.

Overall, the proposed vision considers the following:

1. **Automated behavior**: 6G IoT systems need to be capable of performing real-time system adaptation, for example, automated, and autonomous integration of new IoT devices, new IoT micro-services in real time or with low latency, while being able to support other types of real-time traffic, for example, high-definition video, AR/VR.
2. **Intelligence on the edge:** ML integration on the far edge requires additional investment in distributed learning approaches beyond federated learning; adaptation of ML models to the edge constrains both in terms of nodes and in terms of network (e.g., mobility and intermittent connectivity).

3. **Decentralized edge computing**: service decentralization is a core aspect of 6G IoT in dense deployments. This requires addressing an adequate support across the edge–cloud continuum, where the networking infrastructure needs to become more flexible, intent, and context-driven, that is, network and computational aspects on edge computing need to be worked as a single system. This requires addressing joint computational and networking paradigms that integrate, by design, aspects such as security, trustworthiness, mobility support, decentralized, and flexible naming spaces and: joint service composition.

4. **Context-awareness**: 6G IoT devices need to integrate some aspects of social behavior, to best serve services such as MCS, and to best operate in dense environments, such as mMTC. For this, there is the need to address network dynamic properties (e.g., degree, reachability, density, etc.) via an interdisciplinary perspective that takes into consideration definitions from computer science and from social sciences.

Acknowledgements

This work has been partially funded by the ICT-56 EU-IoT project, grant nr. 825082.

References

[1] E. Dutkiewicz, X. Costa-Perez, I. K.-I. Network, and undefined 2017, "Massive machine-type communications," ieeexplore.ieee.org.

[2] N. D. Lane, S. B. Eisenman, M. Musolesi, E. Miluzzo, and A. T. Campbell, "Urban Sensing Systems: Opportunistic or Participatory?," Proc. of HotMobile. Napa Valley, USA, Feb-2008.

[3] R. Ganti, F. Ye, H. L.-I. communications Magazine, and undefined 2011, "Mobile crowdsensing: current state and future challenges," ieeexplore.ieee.org.

[4] C. Prandi, V. Nisi, M. Ribeiro, and N. Nunes, "Sensing and making sense of tourism flows and urban data to foster sustainability awareness: a real-world experience," J. Big Data, vol. 8, no. 1, pp. 1–25, Dec. 2021.

[5] G. S. Tuncay, G. Benincasa, and A. Helmy, "Participant recruitment and data collection framework for opportunistic sensing: A Comparative Analysis," Proc. 8th ACM MobiCom Work. Challenged networks - CHANTS '13, no. September, p. 25, 2013.

[6] E. F. Recognition, "Relevance and Cognition for Self-Awareness in a Content-centric Internet Project." [Online]. Available: http://users.cs .cf.ac.uk/Recognition.Project/wordpress/?page_id=36.[Accessed: 18-Jan-2016].

[7] S. T. Moturu, I. Khayal, N. Aharony, W. Pan, and A. Pentland, "Using Social Sensing to Understand the Links between Sleep, Mood, and Sociability," in 2011 IEEE Third International Conference on Privacy, Security, Risk and Trust and 2011 IEEE Third International Conference on Social Computing, 2011, pp. 208–214.

[8] K. K. Rachuri, C. Mascolo, M. Musolesi, and P. J. Rentfrow, "Sociable-Sense: Exploring the Trade-offs of Adaptive Sampling and Computation Offloading for Social Sensing," in Proceedings of the 17th Annual International Conference on Mobile Computing and Networking, 2011, pp. 73–84.

[9] M. N. Burns et al., "Harnessing context sensing to develop a mobile intervention for depression.," J. Med. Internet Res., vol. 13, no. 3, p. e55, Jan. 2011.

[10] L. Jin, Y. Chen, T. Wang, P. Hui, and A. V Vasilakos, "Understanding user behavior in online social networks: a survey," Commun. Mag. IEEE, vol. 51, no. 9, pp. 144–150, Sep. 2013.

[11] H. Ma, D. Zhao, and P. Yuan, "Opportunities in Mobile Crowd Sensing MOBILE CROWD SENSING Opportunities in Mobile Crowd Sensing," 2015.

[12] L. Carvalho, R. S.- IoT, and undefined 2020, "A Review on Scaling Mobile Sensing Platforms for Human Activity Recognition: Challenges and Recommendations for Future Research," mdpi.com.

[13] N. Palaghias, S. A. Hoseinitabatabaei, M. Nati, A. Gluhak, and K. Moessner, "Accurate detection of real-world social interactions with smartphones," in 2015 IEEE International Conference on Communications (ICC), 2015, pp. 579–585.

[14] Y. Vaizman, K. Ellis, and G. Lanckriet, "Recognizing detailed human context in the wild from smartphones and smartwatches," IEEE Pervasive Comput., vol. 16, no. 4, pp. 62–74, 2017.

[15] R. C. Sofia, S. Firdose, L. Amaral Lopes, W. Moreira, and P. Mendes, "NSense: A People-centric, non-intrusive Opportunistic Sensing Tool for Contextualizing Social Interaction (SHORT VERSION UNDER SUBMISSION)," Cope-Siti-Tr-16-02, pp. 1–6, 2016.

[16] L. Foschini et al., "Edge-enabled Mobile Crowdsensing to Support Effective Rewarding for Data Collection in Pandemic Events," Springer, vol. 19, no. 3, Sep. 2021.

[17] S. Kielienyu, B. Kantarci, D. Turgut, S. K.-P. of the 18th ACM, and undefined 2020, "Bridging predictive analytics and mobile crowdsensing for future risk maps of communities against covid-19," dl.acm.org, pp. 37–45, Nov. 2020.

[18] K. Zhang, J. Cao, ... S. M.-... on C. S., and undefined 2021, "Digital Twin Empowered Content Caching in Social-Aware Vehicular Edge Networks," ieeexplore.ieee.org.

[19] D. Li, S. Wang, H. Zhao, X. W.-I. I. of T. Journal, and undefined 2020, "Context-and-Social-Aware Online Beam Selection for mmWave Vehicular Communications," ieeexplore.ieee.org.

[20] R. Zhang, S. Jia, Y. Ma, C. X.-I. Access, and undefined 2020, "Social-aware D2D video delivery method based on mobility similarity measurement in 5G ultra-dense network," ieeexplore.ieee.org.

[21] "Internet of Things Global Standards Initiative." [Online]. Available: https://www.itu.int/en/ITU-T/gsi/iot/Pages/default.aspx.[Accessed: 10-Dec-2021].

[22] B. Zhang et al., "The Cloud is Not Enough: Saving IoT from the Cloud," Usenix HotStorage 2015, 2015.

[23] T. Mai, H. Yao, S. Guo, Y. L.-I. Network, and undefined 2020, "In-Network Computing Powered Mobile Edge: Toward High Performance Industrial IoT," ieeexplore.ieee.org.

[24] Q. Ju, G. Sun, H. Li, Y. Z.-2018 I. 88th Vehicular, and undefined 2018, "Latency-aware in-network computing for Internet of battery-less things," ieeexplore.ieee.org.

[25] R. C. Sofia and J. Soldatos, "A Vision on Smart , Decentralised Edge Computing Research Directions," NGIoT White Pap., no. September, 2021.

[26] M. Iorga, L. Feldman, R. Barton, M. J. Martin, N. Goren, and C. Mahmoudi, "Fog computing conceptual model," Gaithersburg, MD, Mar. 2018.

[27] J. Ren, D. Zhang, S. He, Y. Zhang, and T. Li, "A survey on end-edge-cloud orchestrated network computing paradigms: Transparent computing, mobile edge computing, fog computing, and cloudlet," ACM Computing Surveys, vol. 52, no. 6. Association for Computing Machinery, pp. 1–36, 01-Oct-2019.

[28] N. Abbas, Y. Zhang, A. Taherkordi, and T. Skeie, "Mobile Edge Computing: A Survey," IEEE Internet Things J., vol. 5, no. 1, pp. 450–465, 2018.

[29] J. Blanch, L. Cicchelli, R. C. Sofia, D. Singl, O. Tirat, and D. Zeghlache, "The Need for Network Service Composition in GAIA-X," GAIA-X position paper, 2021. [Online]. Available: https://www.google.com/sea rch?q=+The+Need+for+Network+Service+Composition+in+GAIA-X &client=firefox-b-d&ei=pk6zYb34A7-I9u8P6IKd0A4&ved=0ahUK Ewi949WWpNn0AhU_hP0HHHWhBB-oQ4dUDCA0&uact=5&oq=+T he+Need+for+Network+Service+Composition+in+GAIA-X&gs_lcp=C gdnd3Mtd2l.[Accessed:10-Dec-2021].

[30] S. Greengard, "AI on edge," Commun. ACM, vol. 63, no. 9, pp. 18–20, Aug. 2020.

[31] R. Marculescu, D. Marculescu, and U. Ogras, "Edge AI: Systems Design and ML for IoT Data Analytics," Proc. ACM SIGKDD Int. Conf. Knowl. Discov. Data Min., pp. 3565–3566, Aug. 2020.

[32] R. C. Sofia, L. I. Carvalho, and F. de M. Pereira, "The Role of Smart Data in Inference of Human Behavior and Interaction," in "Smart Data: State-of-the-Art and Perspectives in Computing and Applications". Group, USA. April 2019., K.-C. Li, Q. Z. L. T. Yang, and B. Di Martino., Eds. CRC Press, Taylor & Francis, 2018.

[33] J. Faraway, N. A.-S. & P. Letters, and undefined 2018, "When small data beats big data," Elsevier, 2017.

[34] L. Dutta, S. B.-I. of Things, and undefined 2021, "TinyML Meets IoT: A Comprehensive Survey," Elsevier.

[35] P. Warden and D. Situnayake, TinyML. 2019.

[36] P. Hui, J. Crowcroft, and E. Yoneki, "BUBBLE Rap: Social-Based Forwarding in Delay-Tolerant Networks," IEEE Trans. Mob. Comput., vol. 10, no. 11, pp. 1576–1589, 2011.

[37] A. Mtibaa, M. May, M. Ammar, and C. Diot, "PeopleRank: Combining Social and Contact Information for Opportunistic Forwarding," in IEEE INFOCOM 2010 MiniConference, 2010.

[38] M. C. Gonzalez C. A. Hidalgo and A.-L. Barabasi, "Understanding individual human mobility patterns," Nature, vol. 453, no. 7, pp. 779–782.

[39] V. Borrel, F. Legendre, M. Dias de Amorim, and S. Fdida, "SIMPS: Using Sociology for Personal Mobility," IEEE/ACM Trans. Netw., vol. 17, no. 3, pp. 831–842, Jun. 2009.

[40] A. Ribeiro and R. Sofia, "A Survey on Mobility Models for Wireless Networks," Feb. 2011.

[41] S. Chao, H. Lee, ... C. C.-I. communications, and undefined 2013, "Bio-inspired proximity discovery and synchronization for D2D communications," ieeexplore.ieee.org.

[42] S. Wasserman and K. Faust, Social network analysis: Methods and applications, vol. 8. Cambridge university press, 1994.

[43] R. Reagans, "Close Encounters: Analyzing How Social Similarity and Propinquity Contribute to Strong Network Connections," Organ. Sci., vol. 22, no. 4, pp. 835–849, Aug. 2011.

[44] A. Clauset, M. E. J. Newman, and C. Moore, "Finding community structure in very large networks," Phys. Rev. E, vol. 70, no. 6, p. 66111, Dec. 2004.

[45] M. E. J. Newman, "The Structure and Function of Complex Networks," SIAM Rev., vol. 45, no. 2, pp. 167–256, Jan. 2003.

[46] J. K.- Society, undefined April, and undefined 2002, "Could it be a big world after all? The six degrees of separation myth," cs.princeton.edu.

[47] S. Milgram, "The Small World Problem," 1967. [Online]. Available: http://measure.igpp.ucla.edu/GK12-SEE-LA/Lesson_Files_09/Tina_Wey/TW_social_networks_Milgram_1967_small_world_problem.pdf .[Accessed:18-Jan-2016].

[48] D. J. Watts and S. H. Strogatz, "Collective dynamics of 'small-world' networks.," Nature, vol. 393, no. 6684, pp. 440–2, Jun. 1998.

[49] A. Lancichinetti and S. Fortunato, "Community detection algorithms: A comparative analysis," Phys. Rev. E, vol. 80, no. 5, p. 56117, Nov. 2009.

[50] F. Murtagh, P. C.-W. I. R. Data, and undefined 2012, "Algorithms for hierarchical clustering: an overview," Wiley Online Libr., vol. 2, no. 1, pp. 86–97, Jan. 2011.

[51] R. S. Burt, "Positions in networks," Soc. forces, vol. 55, no. 1, pp. 93–122, 1976.

[52] R. Tarjan, "Depth-first search and linear graph algorithms," SIAM J. Comput., vol. 1, no. 2, pp. 146–160, 1972.

[53] M. C. Gonzalez, C. A. Hidalgo, and A.-L. Barabasi, "Understanding individual human mobility patterns," Nature, vol. 453, no. 7196, pp. 779–782, Jun. 2008.

[54] C. Song, Z. Qu, N. Blumm, and A.-L. Barabási, "Limits of predictability in human mobility.," Science, vol. 327, no. 5968, pp. 1018–1021, Feb. 2010.

[55] M. Musolesi and C. Mascolo, "A community based mobility model for ad hoc network research," in REALMAN '06: Proceedings of the second international workshop on Multi-hop ad hoc networks: from theory to reality, 2006, pp. 31–38.

[56] V. Borrel, F. Legendre, M. de Amorim, and S. Fdida, "{SIMPS}: Using Sociology for Personal Mobility," IEEE/ACM Trans. Netw., vol. 17, no. 3, pp. 831–842, Jun. 2009.

6

An Introduction to Quantum Imaging and Hologram

Kwang-Cheng Chen and Joseph McElroy

Kwang-Chen Cheng, University of South Florida, FL, USA,
Joseph McElroy, University of South Florida, Tampa, FL, USA,
E-mail: kwangcheng@usf.edu

Abstract

After Bell resolved the famous argument between A. Einstein and Copenhagen school about quantum entanglement, possible applications of quantum mechanics to information technology have become materialized. Starting from a brief mathematical treatment of quantum entanglement, the principles of quantum imaging and quantum holography will be presented for better quality over the limitation of traditional engineering technology, with state-of-the-art literature review regarding this major advance of imaging technology that may greatly advance in medical imaging and the AR/VR technology in metaverse that is a primary new application of 6G communications.

Keywords: Quantum Imaging, Quantum Hologram, Quantum Entanglement, Quantum Optical Information Processing, AR, VR, Metaverse.

6.1 Introduction

After the advancement of classic mechanics, electromagnetic theory (i.e., Maxwell equations), and statistical mechanics, modern physics was coming to the stage while getting into the twentieth century [1]. There existed three major dilemmas of classic physics:

- Blackbody radiation: Considering a blackbody, the classic physics could not find a good explanation of the radiation spectrum from it. Max Planck proposed the concept of quanta with a clump of energy $E = hf$ or its multiple, to well explain the radiation spectrum, while h is known as the *Planck constant*. It is considered as the birth of quantum mechanics.
- Photoelectronic effect: When light shines on the surface of a metallic substance, electrons in the metal absorb the energy of the light and they can escape from the metal's surface. Classic physics expects that when using very dim light, it would take some time for enough light energy to build up to eject an electron from a metallic surface. However, experiments show that if light of a certain frequency can eject electrons from a metal, it makes no difference in the strength of the light. There is never a time delay. This dilemma was solved by A. Einstein leading to his Nobel prize.
- Hydrogen atom: It is known that the nucleus of a hydrogen atom carries the positive charge and the electron circling the nucleus carries the negative charge. The hydrogen atom is supposed to collapse due to the electrical attraction almost immediately, but actually not. Bohr proposed the idea that the electron evolves to satisfy the relation of $m_e vr = n\hbar$, where $\hbar = h/2\pi$.

The double-split experiment shown in Figure 6.1 suggests another puzzle. It was widely considered photons and electrons as particles. If so, the double-split experiment is supposed to have the result as the upper half of the figure. However, the experimental outcomes exhibit the lower half of the figure to suggest the nature of wave. This is known as the *wave-particle duality*. Louis de Broglie developed the theory to explain duality of the matter and wave.

Werner Heisenberg further proposed the *uncertainty principle* with the famous inequality (shown in one-dimension)

$$\Delta\sigma_x \Delta\sigma_p \geq \hbar/2, \tag{6.1}$$

which indicates that the error to measure the position of a particle and the error to measure the momentum of a particle is greater than a constant. Uncertainty principle plays fundamental role in quantum mechanics, which suggests the impossibility to precise measure the position (and thus state) of a tiny particle such as an electron and a photon. It is quite different from what we expect in classic physics.

The next milestone in quantum mechanics is the Schrödinger equation that opens the door of wave mechanics to describe the mechanics of particles,

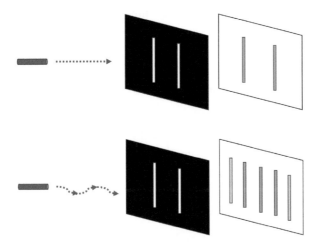

Figure 6.1 Instead of the nature of particles, the double-split experiment leads to the nature of wave for photons or electrons.

on top of the Hamiltonian (the sum of kinetic energy and potential), which is

$$-\frac{\hbar^2}{2m}\nabla^2\psi + V\psi = E\psi, \tag{6.2}$$

where ψ is statistically interpreted by Max Born as a probability distribution. Up to this point, quantum mechanics demonstrate quite different formulation and physical view than classic mechanics. In order to understand Quantum Mechanics in more depth, further mathematical tools have to be employed.

6.1.1 Dirac's notations

In Quantum Mechanics, where systems are elitely defined on a Hilbert space, vectors are indicated with a special notation, introduced by Dirac, another Nobel laureate. Throughout this chapter, we will use Dirac's notations to describe the principles of quantum computing, information processing, and communications [2].

A vector x of a Hilbert space $\mathbb{H}$ is interpreted as a *column vector*, of possibly infinite dimension, and is indicated by the symbol $|x\rangle$ which is called *ket*. Its transpose conjugate $|x\rangle^*$ should be interpreted as a *row vector*, and is represented by the symbol

$$\langle x| = |x\rangle^*, \tag{6.3}$$

which is called *bra*. As a consequence, the inner product of two vectors $|x\rangle$ and $|y\rangle$ is indicated in the form

$$\langle x|y\rangle. \tag{6.4}$$

Example: Suppose the vector u is

$$u = \begin{pmatrix} u_1 \\ u_2 \\ u_3 \end{pmatrix} = |u\rangle. \tag{6.5}$$

Then, its complex conjugate is

$$\langle u| = (u_1^*, u_2^*, u_3^*). \tag{6.6}$$

Consequently, their inner product is

$$\langle u|u\rangle = \|u_1\|^2 + \|u_2\|^2 + \|u_3\|^2 = \|u\|^2, \tag{6.7}$$

which is the L^2 norm.

A linear combination of vectors is written as the form

$$|x\rangle = a_1|x_1\rangle + a_2|x_2\rangle + \cdots + a_n|x_n\rangle. \tag{6.8}$$

The norm of a vector is written as $\|x\| = \sqrt{\langle x|x\rangle}$. The orthogonality condition between two vectors $|x\rangle$ and $|y\rangle$ is now written as

$$\langle x|y\rangle = 0,$$

and the orthonormality of a basis $\mathcal{U} = \{|b\rangle_i, i \in I\}$ is written in the form

$$\langle b_i|b_j\rangle = \delta_{ij}.$$

The Fourier expansion with a finite-dimensional orthonormal basis $\mathcal{U} = \{|b\rangle_i, i = 1, \cdots, n\}$ becomes

$$|x\rangle = a_1|b_1\rangle + \cdots + a_n|b_n\rangle, \tag{6.9}$$

where

$$a_i = \langle b_i|x\rangle,$$

and can also be written in the form

$$|x\rangle = \langle b_1 \mid x\rangle)|b\rangle_1 + \cdots + \langle b_n \mid x\rangle |b_n\rangle. \tag{6.10}$$

Example (Fourier Series): Please recall the Fourier series to expand a function $g(t)$ on the finite-dimension basis $\{e^{-j2\pi kft}\}_{k=1}^{n}$. This situation exactly corresponds to eqn (6.9) by

$$g(t) \longleftrightarrow x$$
$$e^{-j2\pi kft} \longleftrightarrow |b_k\rangle,$$

where $\langle b_k|g\rangle, k = 1, ..., n$ correspond to the coefficients of Fourier series. $|x\rangle \langle y|$ denote the outer product in matrix form. Say,

$$|x\rangle = \begin{pmatrix} x_1 \\ x_2 \end{pmatrix} \quad |y\rangle = \begin{pmatrix} y_1 \\ y_2 \end{pmatrix}.$$

Then,

$$|x\rangle \langle y| = \begin{pmatrix} x_1 y_1 & x_1 y_2 \\ x_2 y_1 & x_2 y_2 \end{pmatrix}. \tag{6.11}$$

▶**Exercise:** Consider two-dimensional vectors and let us define

$$|0\rangle = \begin{pmatrix} 1 \\ 0 \end{pmatrix} \quad |1\rangle = \begin{pmatrix} 0 \\ 1 \end{pmatrix}.$$

Please find $|0\rangle \langle 0|, |0\rangle \langle 1|, |1\rangle \langle 0|, |1\rangle \langle 1|$.
▶**Exercise:** If

$$|x\rangle = \begin{pmatrix} x_{11} & x_{12} \\ x_{21} & x_{22} \end{pmatrix} \quad |y\rangle = \begin{pmatrix} y_1 \\ y_2 \\ y_3 \end{pmatrix}.$$

Please find $|x\rangle \langle y|$.

6.1.2 Quantum states

After successful statistical interpretation of Schrödinger equation, Schrödinger raised a famous philosophy question that is known as *Schrödinger's cat* illustrated in Figure 6.2. Suppose we put a cat into a box for weeks without the food and water (sorry, we should love animals). Without opening the box, this cat might be dead or still alive but extremely weak. The "state" of this cat in the box is therefore a mixture of state "dead" and state "alive". However, once we open the box, which represents a kind of measurement, the state of this cat is either dead or alive. It is suggested that such mixture can be viewed as a

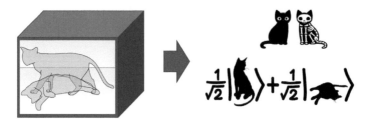

Figure 6.2   Schrödinger's cat.

kind of superposition to form the concept of quantum states, though Einstein disagreed such a concept.

Such a superposition can be viewed in wave functions or in probabilistic/statistical functions.

Quantum computing, information processing, and communications deal with the quantum states. The most straightforward quantum state considers the polarization of a photon. Two common polarizations of a photon is horizontal that is denoted by $|\rightarrow\rangle$ or $|H\rangle$, and vertical $|\uparrow\rangle$ or $|V\rangle$. These two polarizations can form an orthonormal basis $\{|\rightarrow\rangle, |\uparrow\rangle\}$ or $\{|H\rangle, |V\rangle\}$. Consequently, a quantum state $|\psi\rangle$ can be defined as

$$|\psi\rangle = \alpha |\rightarrow\rangle + \beta |\uparrow\rangle, \tag{6.12}$$

where $\|\alpha\|^2 + \|\beta\|^2 = 1$, $\alpha, \beta \in \mathbb{C}$.

Example: Similarly, a different way to view polarizations can form another basis $\{|\nearrow\rangle, |\nwarrow\rangle\}$, we can intuitively obtain

$$|\uparrow\rangle = \frac{1}{\sqrt{2}}(|\nearrow\rangle + |\nwarrow\rangle) \tag{6.13}$$

$$|\rightarrow\rangle = \frac{1}{\sqrt{2}}(|\nearrow\rangle - |\nwarrow\rangle), \tag{6.14}$$

where $\frac{1}{\sqrt{2}}$ is for the purpose of normalization.

Remark: There are many ways to create the basis for the quantum states. However, the polarization serves as the primary consideration in the following chapters, in case no special claim. Furthermore, it is possible to have more than two orthonormal components in a basis as we will see later.

By the above definition of quantum states on the polarization of a photon, it is natural to define a *qubit*, that is a binary quantum bit, to represent "0" and "1" in a binary quantum system. For the simplicity of notations, such two quantum states can be denoted as $|0\rangle$ and $|1\rangle$, without the need of specifying the physical realization of these quantum states.

Remark: It is possible to develop quantum states beyond binary, but we will primarily focus on single-qubit and multiple-qubit systems later this chapter.

6.2 Quantum Entanglement

The argument of Schrödinger's cat leads to the concept of probabilistic super-position of quantum states, which again totally differs from classic physics. Hereafter, we start from *quantum superposition* and then initially explore *quantum entanglement* that goes beyond the intuition of classic physics.

6.2.1 Quantum superposition and entanglement

In a classic system of two possible states, such a system is in either one state or another, and can never be simultaneously in both states. For example, your smartphone is either on or off. However, a quantum system can be in the coherent superposition of states [1]. For example, a photon is polarized at an angle θ, with respect to the horizontal, and can be written as in Dirac's ket-bra notation

$$|\theta\rangle = \cos\theta \, |\rightarrow\rangle + \sin\theta \, |\uparrow\rangle . \tag{6.15}$$

That is, the photon simultaneously exists in both horizontal and vertical states of polarizations. Generally speaking, we can denote ψ as the state of a quantum system with binary basis $|1\rangle$ and $|0\rangle$

$$|\psi\rangle = \alpha \, |0\rangle + \beta \, |1\rangle , \tag{6.16}$$

where

$$|\alpha|^2 + |\beta|^2 = 1. \tag{6.17}$$

It can be generalized beyond the binary cases as the *Born's rule* that the sum of squares of the amplitudes of all possible states in the superposition is equal to 1.

Remark: A quantum system with states modeled by two-dimensional vectors can be used as the fundamental information units of computations, which is known as *qubits*. Similarly, three-values quantum information units are called *qutrits* and n-valued quantum information units are called *qudits*.

The equation (6.16) can be viewed with the aid of the *Bloch sphere* shown in Figure 6.3 to intuitively explain quantum operations. A quantum state can be any point on the unitary Bloch sphere. Along the z-axis, $|1\rangle$ and $|0\rangle$ are placed at the two ends. The x-axis indicates a $\pi/2$ formation of $|1\rangle$ and $|0\rangle$. Further rotation $\pi/2$ gives y-axis.

There are many ways to facilitate the binary quantum basis functions. Without particular mention, we consider that a single photon is represented as the superposition of two optical modes, say two polarization modes, due to its straightforward implementation with precision. For example, $|1\rangle$ and $|0\rangle$ can be viewed as $|\rightarrow\rangle$ and $|\uparrow\rangle$ representing two optical polarization modes. Of course, there are many ways to realize $|1\rangle$ and $|0\rangle$.

Remark: Quantum mechanics could successfully model the interaction between a photon and a polaroid that has a preferred polarization. When a photon of the quantum state $|\psi\rangle = \alpha|\uparrow\rangle + \beta|\rightarrow\rangle$ as (6.16) interacts with a polaroid preferred $|\uparrow\rangle$, the photon will get through with probability $|\alpha|^2$ and will be absorbed with probability $|\beta|^2$.

Remark: Multiplying a unitary constant does not change a quantum state vector, but the relative phase in a superposition does represent a distinct quantum state. That is, although $|u_1\rangle \sim e^{i\theta}|u_1\rangle$ (i.e., equivalence), $\frac{1}{\sqrt{2}}(|u_1\rangle + |u_2\rangle)$ and $\frac{1}{\sqrt{2}}(e^{i\theta}|u_1\rangle + |u_2\rangle)$ do not represent the same state.

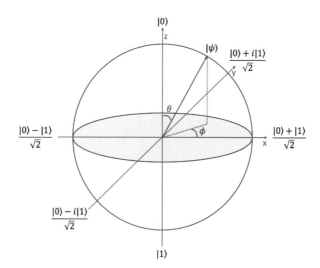

Figure 6.3   The Bloch sphere.

Please find two other widely-used notations for the Bloch sphere, shown in Figure 6.4, by indicating the properties of Bloch sphere. The concept of Bloch sphere is very useful to characterize quantum states, particularly for quantum logic gates and implementation of quantum computers.

Remark: The left version of the Bloch sphere in Figure 6.4 introduces a common set of symbols:

$$|+\rangle = \frac{1}{\sqrt{2}}(|0\rangle + |1\rangle), \tag{6.18}$$

$$|-\rangle = \frac{1}{\sqrt{2}}(|0\rangle - |1\rangle), \tag{6.19}$$

$$|i\rangle = \frac{1}{\sqrt{2}}(|0\rangle + i\,|1\rangle), \tag{6.20}$$

$$|-i\rangle = \frac{1}{\sqrt{2}}(|0\rangle - i\,|1\rangle), \tag{6.21}$$

where the basis $\{|+\rangle, |-\rangle\}$ is referred as the *Hadamard basis*. If we focus on the polarizations of a photon, we sometimes use $\{|\nearrow\rangle, |\nwarrow\rangle\}$ to denote the Hadamard basis.

▶**Exercise:** Dina understood that $|1\rangle$ and $-|1\rangle$ represent the same quantum state. However, $\frac{1}{\sqrt{2}}(|0\rangle + |1\rangle)$ and $\frac{1}{\sqrt{2}}(|0\rangle - |1\rangle)$ do not represent the same quantum state. Please explain the reason to help her.

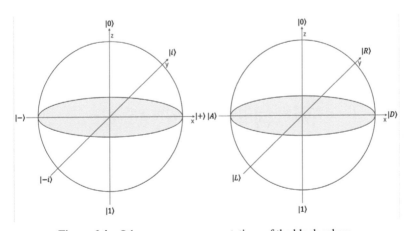

Figure 6.4   Other common representations of the bloch sphere.

Now, let us look further into the difference between a classic system and a quantum system. If a blue ball and a red ball form a classic system and these two balls are distant, the possession of the red ball has absolutely has no affect on the blue ball, and vice versa.

On the other hand, in a quantum system of two photons A, B, we have

$$|\psi_{AB}\rangle = \frac{1}{\sqrt{2}}(|\rightarrow_A\rangle |\uparrow_B\rangle + |\uparrow_A\rangle |\rightarrow_B\rangle). \tag{6.22}$$

Let these two photons be separated in a long distance such that they can not interact each other. Suppose photon A with Alice and photon B with Bob. If Alice measures her photon in state $|\rightarrow_A\rangle$, then Bob's photon is definitely in state $|\uparrow_B\rangle$, vice versa. However, if Alice decides to measure her photon in the basis $\{|\nearrow\rangle, |\nwarrow\rangle\}$ by passing the photon through a polarizer oriented at $45°$ with respect to the horizontal. Recall

$$|\uparrow\rangle = \frac{1}{\sqrt{2}}(|\nearrow\rangle + |\nwarrow\rangle). \tag{6.23}$$

$$|\rightarrow\rangle = \frac{1}{\sqrt{2}}(|\nearrow\rangle - |\nwarrow\rangle). \tag{6.24}$$

The two-photon state becomes

$$|\psi_{AB}\rangle = \frac{1}{\sqrt{2}} [|\nearrow\rangle_A(|\uparrow\rangle_B + |\rightarrow\rangle_B) + |\nwarrow\rangle_A(|\rightarrow\rangle_B - |\uparrow\rangle_B)]. \tag{6.25}$$

Consequently, the measurement outcome of Alice's photon in the state $|\nearrow_A\rangle$ is

$$\langle \nearrow_A|\psi_{AB}\rangle = \frac{1}{\sqrt{2}}(|\uparrow_B\rangle + |\rightarrow_B\rangle) = |\nearrow_B\rangle. \tag{6.26}$$

On the other hand, if Alice's photon is measured in the state $|\nwarrow_A\rangle$

$$\langle \nwarrow_A|\psi_{AB}\rangle = \frac{1}{\sqrt{2}}(|\uparrow_B\rangle - |\rightarrow_B\rangle) = -|\nwarrow_B\rangle. \tag{6.27}$$

Therefore, the quantum state of Bob's photon depends on what Alice decides to do, while there is no way for Alice's photon and Bob's photon to interact with each other. Similarly, the state of Alice's photon is influenced by what Bob does to his photon. That is, these two photons are *entangled* even if they are too far apart to interact, due to the fact that these two photons are initially created in a *non-separable* quantum state as (6.22).

Remark: The state of AB system is *separable* if $|\psi_{AB}\rangle = |\psi_A\rangle |\psi_B\rangle$.

Example: Suppose we have the quantum state of two photons as follows:

$$|\psi\rangle_{AB} = \frac{1}{\sqrt{2}}(|\uparrow_A\rangle |\uparrow_B\rangle + |\uparrow_A\rangle |\rightarrow_B\rangle). \tag{6.28}$$

$$= |\uparrow_A\rangle \left[\frac{1}{\sqrt{2}}(|\uparrow_B\rangle + |\rightarrow_B\rangle) \right]. \tag{6.29}$$

The quantum state of photons A and B are separable.

Example: Suppose we have the quantum state of two photons as follows:

$$|\psi\rangle_{AB} = \frac{1}{\sqrt{2}}(|\uparrow_A\rangle |\rightarrow_B\rangle + |\rightarrow_A\rangle |\uparrow_B\rangle). \tag{6.30}$$

The quantum state of photons A and B are non-separable, which suggests an entangled state.

6.2.2 Optical realization of quantum entanglement

There are many ways to generate entangled photons or particles. The most well-known technique to generate entangled photon pairs might be *spontaneous parametric down-conversion* (SPDC), while Figure 6.5 illustrates a kind of realization.

Generally speaking, a nonlinear crystal is used to split the photon beam into pairs of photons, following the laws of conservation of energy or momentum. Different types of SPDC can be categorized by the polarizations of the input photons from the pump laser and the output paired photons (signal and idler). If the signal and idler photons are of the same polarization but orthogonal to the polarization of pump laser, it is type I SPDC. If the polarizations of signal and idler photons are orthogonal, it is type II SPDC.

The basic principle of *beam splitter* can be understood in the following way. Suppose two photons are incident from a as shown in Figure 6.6. The incident quantum state can be represented by

$$|\psi_{in}\rangle = |a_1\rangle |a_2\rangle.$$

Applying the beam splitter gives

$$|a_1\rangle |a_2\rangle \longrightarrow \frac{1}{2}(|c_1\rangle + i |d_1\rangle)(|c_2\rangle + i |d_2\rangle). \tag{6.31}$$

$$= \frac{1}{2}(|c_1\rangle |c_2\rangle + i |c_1\rangle |d_2\rangle + i |c_2\rangle |d_1\rangle - |d_1\rangle |d_2\rangle). \tag{6.32}$$

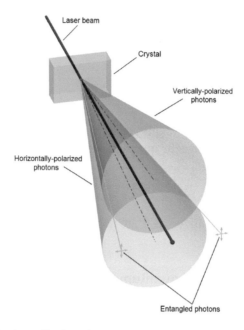

Figure 6.5   An realization of SPDC with output type II (from Wikipedia).

If we conduct quantum measurements at c and d, then

$$P(\text{both photons in c}) = 1/4$$
$$P(\text{both photons in d}) = 1/4$$
$$P(\text{one photon each at c and d}) = 1/2$$

which means that photons go to c and d with the same probability.

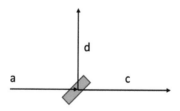

Figure 6.6   A beam splitter: incident from a and outputs at c and d.

6.3 Quantum Imaging

Quantum entanglement is not only useful in the new frontier of computing and communications, but many novel applications such as quantum metrology and quantum information processing, which has been overlooked for the potential of commercial engineering. By looking into the spirit of quantum entanglement and non-locality, extremely high correlation of photons and even light beams may suggest phenomenon and mechanisms beyond the view of classic world. In this section, quantum imaging is introduced and typically realized by the interferometer that has been used to generate entangled photons, with special interest as *ghost imaging* (GI).

Correlated-photon imaging, or ghost imaging, is an interferometric method for (potentially nonlocally) imaging an object using (at least) two beams of light, one which interacts with the object, and one which does not. This can be done with a weaker classical correlation or an entangled correlation created via spontaneous parametric down-conversion (SPDC). Erkman and Shapiro described it as acquisition of an object's transmittance pattern by means of intensity correlation measurements [3]. The nonlocality that GI enables has fascinating implications using wireless optical beams. It is possible to deploy lower-sensitivity photo-detectors in the field, while laboratory-grade equipment could be used to generate the images remotely [4]. A typical interferer realization of ghost imaging is illustrated in Figure 6.7.

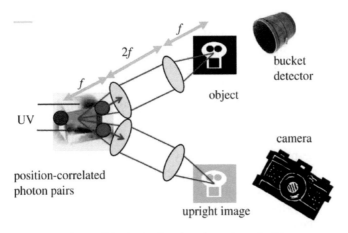

Figure 6.7 Basic ghost imaging schematic [6].

The intuition of quantum imaging is to take advantage of high correlation similar to quantum entanglement. Therefore, the realization is not necessarily through quantum optics. To enrich the quality of quantum imaging, more effective carrier of bits emerges as an important technique, which is also useful in quantum optical communications. Orbital angular momentum was shown almost 30 years ago to characterize light down to the single photon level for potentially higher bandwidth of transmitted data per optical beam or photon. This discovery unleashed a flurry of research as the potential and difficulties of using this approach became evident. While a theoretically unlimited amount of information per photon can be encoded, the fragility of the state increases proportionally, and turbulence in free space can then destroy the information. However, the successful transmission of more data or via fewer photons could enrich the imaging quality or save a lot of transmission energy.

Quantum imaging is to find means to outperform classical imaging systems while overcomes the shot noise and the standard quantum limits, and enhances applications like through-wall imaging, medical imaging, and detection of targets using more advanced camouflaging techniques.

6.4 Quantum Hologram

Holography allows the reconstruction of the 3-D spatial information of an object through amplitude and phase information from the light reflected from that object. A further quantum imaging technology is called *quantum holography*, which takes advantage of entangled-photon pairs in two scatters. One scatter from the remote object, while another scatter through local conventional optics to offer full spatial resolution. Quantum entanglement amazingly enables the measurement to yield coherent holographic information regarding the remote object without any optical observation about the object.

Figure 6.8 depicts the fundamental realization of quantum holography. S is the source of entangled-photon pairs. C denotes a remote single-photon sensitive sphere that conceals a hidden object. D indicates a local two-dimensional single-photon-sensitive array detector. h_1 and h_2 represent the optical systems to deliver the entangled photons in respective directions of $S \rightarrow C$ and $S \rightarrow D$. Based on the information $C \rightarrow D$, the quantity $\bar{p}_2(\mathbf{x}_2)$ is known as the marginal coincidence rate, which can indirectly regenerate the hologram of the concealed object while the lines in time represent optical and consequent electrical signals.

At the beginning of this section, holography and Figure 6.8 requires illumination on the target object. In [11], it is shown that quantum hologram can be formed even without detecting the light on the target object. Figure 6.9 illustrates the experimental setup to verify the technology. Laser light in purple pumps the nonlinear crystal (i.e., ppKTP) into beams in path *a* and path *d*, which forms the signal beam in red and the idler beam in green, in the forward direction of path *b* and path *c* or backward direction of path *e*

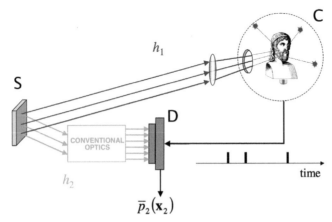

Figure 6.8 Quantum holography [10].

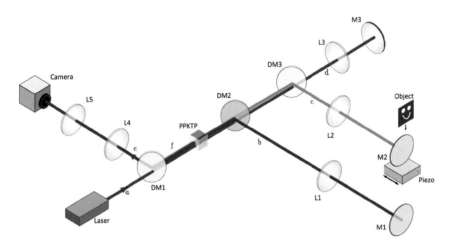

Figure 6.9 Quantum holography without detected light [11].

and path f. The (Dichroic) mirrors (i.e., DM1, DM2, and DM3) separate the different beam paths. Idler light beam illuminates the object in path c, while its hologram can be detected on the camera with signal light beam of path e. The mirrors (i.e., M1, M2, and M3) function as the end mirrors of the interferometer, while M2 can precisely move in one direction. In this setup, entangled or highly correlated signal and idler photon pairs are used in a nonlinear interferometer to obtain a hologram of the idler photon, through measurement of the signal photon.

As the report of *IEEE Spectrum* in February 2022, quantum hologram as an indirect imaging can be formed to provide a three-dimensional scene without the need of *seeing* (i.e., capturing the light from) the object. The potential applications are broad, particularly in biomedical areas or to enhance AR/VR technology in metaverse that is a major new applications of 6G mobile communications..

Acknowledgements

The first author appreciates the teaching and research support from the Quantum Initiatives and the research support from the Institute of Applied Engineering, University of South Florida.

References

[1] M. S. Zubairy, *Quantum Mechanics for Beginners*, Cambridge University Press, 2020.

[2] E. Rieffel, W. Polak, "An Introduction to Quantum Computing for Non-Physicists", *ACM Computing Suveys*, vol. 32, no. 3, pp. 300-335, Sep. 2000.

[3] Baris I. Erkmen, Jeffrey H. Shapiro, "Ghost Imaging: What is quantum, what is not", 2007. https://arxiv.org/abs/quant-ph/0612070.

[4] D. Simon, G. Jaeger, S. Gregg, V. Alexander, *Quantum Metrology, Imaging, and Communication*, Springer International Publishing, DOI 10.1007/978-3-319-46551-7.

[5] Baris, Ilayda and Shapiro, Jeffrey, "Ghost imaging: From quantum to classical to computational", *Advances in Optics and Photonics*, vol. 2, pp. 405-450. 10.1364/AOP.2.000405, 2010.

[6] Padgett, Miles and Boyd, Robert. (2017). An introduction to ghost imaging: Quantum and classical. Philosophical Transactions of The

Royal Society A Mathematical Physical and Engineering Sciences. 375. 20160233.

[7] Shih, Yanhua. (2008). The Physics of Ghost Imaging. 10.1364/ICQI.2008.QTuB1. https://arxiv.org/abs/0805.1166.

[8] Preskill, John. Course Information for Physics 219/Computer Science 219 Quantum Computation (Formerly Physics 229). 2019. https://web. archive.org/web/20190206073136/http://theory.caltech.edu/people/pr eskill/ph219/.Specifically,seeChapter10:QuantumShannonTheory(pg.2 5). 2016. https://authors.library.caltech.edu/66493/2/chap10_15.pdf(al ternatedirectlink).

[9] Lanzagorta, Marco and Uhlmann, Jeffrey. (2019). Overview of the Current State of Quantum-Based Technologies. Marine Technology Society Journal. 53. 75-87. 10.4031/MTSJ.53.5.14.

[10] A. F. Abouraddy, B. E. A. Saleh, A. V. Sergienko, M. C. Teich, "Quantum Holography", *Optical Express*, vol. 9, no. 10, November 5, 2001.

[11] S. Topfer, M. G. Basset, J. F. Steinlechner, J. P. Torres, M. Grafe, "Quantum Holography with Undetected Light", *Science Advances*, vol. 8, no. 2, 2022.

7

Localization of Low Complexity and Low Power Consumption IoRT Terminals

Ernestina Cianca, Mauro De Sanctis, and Tommaso Rossi

Center for Teleinfrastructure (CTIF), University of Rome "Tor Vergata",
Italy
E-mail: cianca@ing.uniroma2.it; mauro.de.sanctis@uniroma2.it;
tommaso.rossi@uniroma2.it

Abstract

This chapter focuses on localization techniques for Internet of Remote Things based on a single satellite, providing information on the achievable performance, and outlining current challenges and relevant research directions.

Keywords: IoRT, IoT, localization, satellites.

7.1 Introduction

The space component will play a key role in enabling the convergence between communication, navigation, and sensing, which is one of the key objectives of 6G. This chapter focuses on the convergence between communication and localization in the specific scenario of the so-called Internet-of-Remote-Things (IoRT) where communication and localization must be performed using low-cost and low-power consumption terminals. The knowledge of the position of the IoRT terminal is important for current and future location-based applications. However, the knowledge of the position of the IoRT terminal is crucial also to ease the integration with 5G and overcome some challenges of the communications with fast-moving LEO satellites such as long and variable delays and high Doppler shifts. Terminal location information in combination with satellite ephemeris data may be used to support mobility, compensate for Doppler effects, and achieve time and frequency synchronization.

As a matter of fact, 3GPP has agreed to assume that user equipments (UEs) will be equipped with a Global Navigation Satellite System (GNSS) receiver. This assumption appears unrealistic in an IoRT scenario where low consumption and low complexity terminals are involved. Therefore, different solutions must be investigated. This chapter provides an overview of localization techniques of IoRT terminals from one single satellite, showing achievable performance and outlining challenges and research directions.

The chapter is organized as follows: Section 7.2 presents satellite IoRT scenarios; Section 7.3 reviews the 5G standard with respect to the integration with NTN, outlining how the knowledge of the position of the UE could be crucial for such an integration; Section 7.4 reviews the geo-localization of RF sources via satellites outlining the challenges that are posed by the IoRT scenarios. Section 7.5 provides an introduction to single satellite geo-localization via TDOA/FDOA. Conclusions are drawn in Section 7.6.

7.2 Satellite IoRT Scenarios

According to recent market studies, the total number of connected IoT devices will reach 83 billion by 2024, rising from 35 billion connections in 2020. The industrial IoT (IIoT) sector including manufacturing, retail, and agriculture, is forecast to account for over 70% of all IoT connections by 2024, with a grow of the number of IIoT units of 180% over the next 4 years [1]. In many of the applications, the IoT devices are distributed over wide and remote geographical areas where terrestrial networks are unavailable or out of reach, such as on remote land (think at the case of areas such , forests) as well as offshore (e.g., in the oceans). In this contexts, a satellite-based connectivity will play a key role. The following, are some of the Internet of Remote Things scenarios.

7.2.1 Agriculture

The production of food must be made more efficient, resource-saving, and ecologically compatible. The possibility to collect data related to the health of soil, moisture analysis, water contamination level, water quantity level and other geodata as well as data on the equipment used on remote fields or on the animals freely moving in the area could be essential to make the agriculture processes more productive, efficient, and environmentally friendly. Moreover, by processing such a data it could be possible to make predictions and better planning for the future.

7.2.2 Environmental monitoring

We can distinguish two types of environmental monitoring applications: the environmental monitoring that refers to the detection of destructive phenomena such as landslides, avalanches, forest fires, volcic eruptions, floods, and earthquakes, and long-term continuous monitoring of air and water pollution, and wildlife position and activity. In both cases, sensors must be place in wide and often remote areas.

7.2.3 Critical infrastructure monitoring

Any accident, malfunctioning, or man-made threat to a critical infrastructure such as railways, gas and oil pipelines and electrical grids poses risk to population safety, and finding a remedy is time-consuming and economically expensive. Continuous monitoring of the long pipelines of gas and oil, the transmission lines of electricity, remote energy generators (winds), the track of railways require coverage in areas that might be non covered by the terrestrial infrastructure and the use of satellite to collect the data will be essential.

In all the mentioned scenarios, the sensors network must be characterized by: large number of nodes, very low cost, ease of deployment, low maintenance, and very long battery duration (possibly using solar energy). Nodes could be highly mobile (i.e., monitoring of wild animals). On the other hand, requirements on communication delay are quite relaxed since this application does not require real-time operation. In this framework, satellites may play a key role, as they would allow to cover a wide area, where the satellite terminal could be also highly mobile, without installing a complex infrastructure. The collection of data from sensors can be done in two ways: (1) direct access and (2) indirect access. In the indirect access mode, each sensor may communicate with the satellite through a sink node the sink which could be provided with a satellite terminal (expensive and power hungry) while the other sensor nodes can be less expensive and power hungry. This solution allows to decrease in the system costs and the complexity of the installation (in terms of antenna pointing and power generation facilities). On the other hand, the direct access to satellite allows much more flexibility, and in the rest of the chapter, we focus on a direct-to-satellite access scenario.

7.3 Location-aided 5G-NTN Integration

Based on the outcome of the Rel-16 study, 3GPP decided to start a work item on NTNs in NR Rel-17. The objective is to specify enhancements necessary for LEO and GEO-based NTNs. The specific characteristics of satellite links, such as e much larger propagation delays and also the variability of the propagation delay along with the much high Doppler shifts, raise the need to modify some of the procedures of 5G-NR standard, especially when LEO satellites are considered. It has been estimated that without compensation, the Doppler shift can be as high as 20 or 24 ppm and the Doppler rate can reach 0.09 and 0.27 ppm/s for an LEO satellite at 600 km. In terrestrial networks, the Doppler shift is mainly related to the UE crystal accuracy which is 10 ppm. Therefore, pre/post-compensation techniques are needed. Currently, the proposed compensation techniques assume [standard]:

- ephemeris knowledge at UE, and
- UEs equipped with a GNSS receiver to know their own position

The larger propagation delays and the high variation of it while the satellite moves, raise the issue to modify the time advance (TA) adjustment. In 5G-NR, the gNodeB provides the UE with a common timing advance (TA) that signals the RTT between the satellite and the gNB. The UE adds the RTT between the UE and the satellite to the TA to get the full TA which is used as an offset between the received downlink timing and uplink transmission timing at the UE. For instance, if downlink slots n starts at time t_1, then the uplink slot n starts at time t_1-full TA. This is important for both random access and data transmissions in connected mode. The problem in this case is twofold:

- the propagation delay is highly variable (the differential delay is 4ms in case of LEO at 600 km and 7 ms in case of LEO at 1500 km) due to the changing distance from UE over Satellite to BS, and hence the TA needs to be dynamically updated;
- The delay, of the order of 28 ms in case of LEO at 600 km and 51 ms in case of 1500 km), is much longer over a satellite link than one TTI (equivalent to one frame), which is equal to or less than 1 ms

The estimation of such TA can be done both at the UE side and at the network (satellite) side but in both cases the knowledge of the UE position is needed.

Handovers is also challenging when LEO constellations are considered. There are different types of hand-overs in Non-Terrestrial networks:

- Intra-satellite handover or spot-beam, which occurs between cells/beams served by the same satellite.
- Inter-satellite handover, or satellite handover, which occurs between cells served by different satellites.
- Inter-technology handover which occurs between terrestrial network access and satellite network access. The handover-triggering mechanism might be asymmetric i.e. leave the satellite network as soon as there is sufficient terrestrial network signal, but only leave the terrestrial network when there is a very low signal.

In NTN systems based on LEO satellites, the cells or spot beams are moving at high speeds and so the handover procedure from one spot beam to the next or from one satellite to the next has to be executed quickly otherwise the UE may not make use of the target beam and/or satellite resources efficiently and in the worst case may suffer the loss of data. From the analysis provided in 3GPP Specification 38.821, it is concluded that handover frequency in LEO NTN can be similar to that experienced by a terrestrial UE on a high-speed train. If the location of the UE is available and it indicates that a handover will occur in a time interval less than a given threshold, then a channel is simultaneously reserved at the satellite selected for the handover and station monitoring is activated by the servicing satellite.

7.4 Geo-location of RF Sources from Satellites

In order to minimize the complexity and the power consumption of IoRT terminals, the capability to estimate (compute) the position of the terminal must be moved to the satellite system using signals transmitted by the IoRT terminals. This is called network-based positioning. Determining the position of a device that transmits RF signals from the Earth is a topic that is gaining more and more attention not only for defence/military purposes. Multiple satellite geo-location techniques using time difference of arrival (TDOA) and frequency difference of arrival (FDOA) measurements are state-of-the-art for interference localization in satellite networks [2]. Also, single satellite geo-location may be carried out using multiple measurements of time and/or frequency over different positions of the satellite.

However, the application scenario in most of the works was rather different: usually, the RF emitter is an interferer with specific characteristics of the waveform; the localization can be also done over longer time (multiple passages of the satellite) and the convergence time is not an issue. Moreover, the performance of such localization algorithms depends also from the involved link budget, type of signals, and protocols that can be used. Only few papers have addressed the specific issue to localize the IoT terminal from an LEO constellation that is designed for communication purposes when the UE is not equipped with GNSS capabilities. In particular, [3] investigates the UT positioning based on the NR synchronization signals in the 5G integrated SatCom systems with multi-beam architecture. Moreover, they propose to design a precoder to optimize the joint synchronization and positioning (JSP) performance of UTs within the whole cell coverage. Chen *et al.* [4] investigate location-based TA estimation for 5G integrated LEO satellite communication systems. They obtain the time difference of arrival (TDOA) and frequency difference of arrival (FDOA) measurements in the downlink timing and frequency synchronization phase, which are made from the satellite at different time instants. They propose to take these measurements for either UE geo-location or ephemeris estimation, thus calculating the TA value. The estimation is then formulated as a quadratic optimization problem whose globally optimal solution can be obtained by a quadratic penalty algorithm. In [5], the access via a GEO satellite is considered and the issue of UE positioning without GNSS receiver is faced considering the limited SNR involved and also the very low duty cycle of the communication. In the next Section, some preliminary results on the trade-off between accuracy and convergence time on the localization from a single satellite using TDOA are shown.

7.4.1 Localization methods

We first recall the TDOA and FDOA principles. Let us use the following notation on a Earth-Centered Earth-Fixed (ECEF) reference system:

- Unknown geographical coordinates of the IoRT terminal: (x, y, z).
- Known geographical coordinates of the ith satellite receivers: (x_i, y_i, z_i).
- Estimate of the distance from the terminal to the ih satellite receiver i: d_i.

Circular positioning systems estimate the location of a source by the intersection of spheres in 3D positioning (or circles in 2D positioning), each sphere representing the locus of points such that the distance d_i from the source to the i-th satellite receiver is constant

$$\begin{cases} \sqrt{(x-x_1)^2 + (y-y_1)^2 + (z-z_1)^2} = d_1 \\ \sqrt{(x-x_2)^2 + (y-y_2)^2 + (z-z_2)^2} = d_2 \\ \dots \end{cases} \quad . \quad (7.1)$$

Taking the time of arrival (TOA) as range estimator, then $d_i = c(T_i - T)$, we have:

$$\begin{cases} \sqrt{(x-x_1)^2 + (y-y_1)^2 + (z-z_1)^2} = c(T_1 - T) \\ \sqrt{(x-x_2)^2 + (y-y_2)^2 + (z-z_2)^2} = c(T_2 - T) \\ \dots \end{cases} \quad . \quad (7.2)$$

where T is the packet transmission time from the source, while T_i is the packet reception time at the i-th satellite receiver.

In order to remove the need to know the value of transmission time T, thus using the TDOA as range estimator, we can take the difference of the circular positioning Equations as a function of the arrival times as follows:

$$\begin{cases} \sqrt{(x-x_1)^2 + (y-y_1)^2 + (z-z_1)^2} + \\ -\sqrt{(x-x_2)^2 + (y-y_2)^2 + (z-z_2)^2} = c(T_1 - T_2) \\ \sqrt{(x-x_1)^2 + (y-y_1)^2 + (z-z_1)^2} + \\ -\sqrt{(x-x_3)^2 + (y-y_3)^2 + (z-z_3)^2} = c(T_1 - T_3) \\ \dots \end{cases} \quad . \quad (7.3)$$

It is worth noting that, assuming a number of N satellite receivers, we can write $N(N-1)/2$ different TDOA Equations (named full TDOA set of Equations), but only $N-1$ Equations are non-redundant (named non-redundant set of TDOA Equations) since $(T_2 - T_3) = (T_1 - T_3) - (T_1 - T_2)$. However, more redundant Equations may be useful to decrease the estimation error when each measurement is affected by noise [5].

Considering the Doppler effect, recall that the received signal frequency f_r of a receiver moving with velocity v for a fixed transmitter using signal frequency f_t is given by:

$$f_r = f_t \left(1 + \frac{v}{c} \cos\theta\right). \quad (7.4)$$

where c is the speed of light and θ is the angle between the vector $\mathbf{v}$ and the Tx-Rx line of sight.

Therefore, assuming a fixed IoRT terminal transmitting at frequency f_t and two satellites moving at speed $\mathbf{v_1}$, $\mathbf{v_2}$ and receiving at frequencies f_1, f_2, FDOA Equations may be written in vector form as follows:

$$c(f_1 - f_2) = -f_t \left[\mathbf{v_1}^T \left(\frac{\mathbf{r_1} - \mathbf{r}}{\|\mathbf{r_1} - \mathbf{r}\|} \right) - \mathbf{v_2}^T \left(\frac{\mathbf{r_2} - \mathbf{r}}{\|\mathbf{r_2} - \mathbf{r}\|} \right) \right], \quad (7.5)$$

Finally, it is worth noting that, as the principle of localization through time or frequency measurements is to use multiple measurements from different satellite positions to solve a system of equations, we may either take measurements from multiple satellites on different positions or take multiple measurements from a single satellite over multiple positions in the orbit. In fact, the above Equations can be applied to the case of a single satellite where the different measurements are taken from the same satellite but in multiple times requiring a longer estimation time.

7.4.2 Illustrative results

In the following, we report some illustrative results of the application of TDOA to a single satellite scenario. We assume the following sources of error:

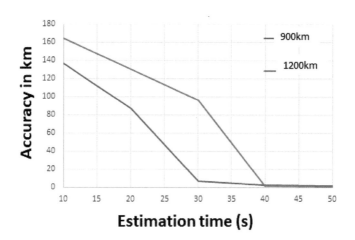

Figure 7.1   Accuracy vs time in case the satellite passes over the emitter.

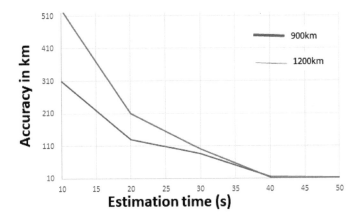

Figure 7.2 Accuracy vs time in case the satellite does not pass over the emitter.

- Standard deviation of the timing measurements, that is, TDOA error= 35 ns.
- Standard deviation of known position of satellite in $x/y/z$, that is, satellite position error=10 m.

Moreover, we consider the satellite at two different altitudes of 900 km and 1200 km. Figures 7.1, 7.2 show the achieved results in case the satellite orbit is such that the satellite passes over the target and in case it does not pass over the target, respectively. As expected the accuracy and the estimation time depends strongly from the geometry and hence, from the position of the satellite with respect to the emitter. Moreover, it is evident that the performance is better in case of lower satellite orbit. However, more deeper studies are needed, considering the specific link budget involved, waveform to perform the timing measurements, and communication protocols.

7.5 Conclusions

This paper has addressed the problem of localizing non-GNSS enabled low-complexity and low-cost IoRT terminals that need to access the satellite for communications purposes.

As the topic of satellite communications supporting IoRT services is more and more attractive, the problem of IoRT terminal localization becomes crucial both for providing location-based services and for providing support to communication protocols, for example, handover algorithms using satellite-fixed-cell or Earth-fixed-cell, paging procedures, carrier recovery with high Doppler shift.

References

[1] M. Centenaro, C. E. Costa, F. Granelli, C. Sacchi, L. Vangelista, A survey on technologies, standards and open challenges in satellite iot, IEEE Communications Surveys Tutorials 23 (3) (2021) 1693–1720. doi: 10.1109/COMST.2021.3078433.

[2] K. Ho, Y. Chan, Solution and performance analysis of geolocation by tdoa, IEEE Transactions on Aerospace and Electronic Systems 29 (4) (1993) 1311–1322. doi:10.1109/7.259534.

[3] T. Chen, W. Wang, R. Ding, G. Seco-Granados, L. You, X. Gao, Precoding design for joint synchronization and positioning in 5g integrated satellite communications, in: 2021 IEEE Global Communications Conference (GLOBECOM), 2021, pp. 01–06. doi:10.1109/GLOBECOM 46510.2021.9685480.

[4] T. Chen, W. Wang, R. Ding, G. Seco-Granados, L. You, X. Gao, Location-based timing advance estimation for 5g integrated leo satellite communications, in: GLOBECOM 2020 - 2020 IEEE Global Communications Conference, 2020, pp. 1–6. doi:10.1109/GLOBECOM42002.2020.932 2428.

[5] C. A. Hofmann, A. Knopp, Tracking of remote iot devices by satellite assisted geolocation, in: ICC 2020 - 2020 IEEE International Conference on Communications (ICC), 2020, pp. 1–6. doi:10.1109/ICC40277.202 0.9149073.

8

Conclusions and Future Scope Perspective

Rute Sofia and Ramjee Prasad

[1]fortiss research institute for software intensive services and systems,
Germany
[2]Ramjee Prasad, CGC, Aarhus University, Denmark
E-mail: sofia@fortiss.org; ramjee@btech.au.dk

The CONASENSE book "Visions for a sustainable and people-centric future" is the product of the CONASENSE 2021 brainstorming workshop and provides an interdisciplinary perspective to the development of 6G, based on the CONASENSE vision, where communications, navigation, sensing, and services need to be articulated together, to build a sustainable, people-centric 6G future.

Starting by challenges and potential technological developments to address as solutions, the book proposes the CONASENSE CNSS architecture, highlighting the role of AI/ML has into the development of a holistic CNSS approach and debating on the potential that quantum ML may bring to provide the required flexibility and speed to the processing of novel 6G services, in particular, Metaverse and XR services.

The book then continues with an international expert perspective on satellite networking, starting with an overview on the status of 5G-NTN integration, and proposing research areas that are relevant in the context of 6G-NTN integration, having in mind the deployment of the 6G-NTN end-to-end infrastructure-as-a-service paradigm.

Aspects such as the current 5G standardization and gNB roles are addressed, proposing also novel architectural advances to support the 6G-NTN integration. Still, within the context of satellite/NTN services, the next chapter provides a set of design choices to devise a suitable 6G-NTN architectural framework, capable of sustaining the operation of dynamic networking services across large-scale multi-orbit satellite constellations. The view concerns the design of a cognitive Service-centric 6G-NTN architecture, where AI/ML is the key to reach flexibility and network adaptation. Such an architecture is expected to be able to support end-to-end services defined by aggregating networking, storage, and computational resources, and orchestrated based on operational intents.

Section 3 provides an overview on the status of IoT, the trend toward service decentralization, and the role of edge computing in this context. Next-generation IoT services are expected to thrive and to be a key set of 6G services to be supported, MCS one such services. Section 4 addresses the current challenges to bring intelligence to the edge in next-generation IoT, as such integration is key to allow 6G IoT deployments to operate in a collectively intelligent way. Section 5 covers principles of social-aware networking, relevant to 6G IoT, explaining how social awareness is today being applied and what are the challenges. Section 5.6 provides recommendations for the integration of an interdisciplinary approach to social awareness in the networking layers, while Section 5.7 concludes the chapter.

Challenges derived from specific 6G services are then addressed, started by the debate on challenges concerning quantum imaging and holograms, expected to be one of the key applications within the 6G Metaverse. Then, another relevant category of 6G services is addressed, IoRT, and localization-aided 5G-NTN integration.

The visions provided in this book by the different experts converge in the following aspects:

- The heterogeneous set of 6G services described requires a look into social behavior, mobility support, and adequate integration of terrestrial and NTN communications.
- AI/ML as a core for supporting an overall cognitive, adaptive, holistic end-to-end infrastructure.
- The need to address the future 6G infrastructure considering an adequate integration of 6G-NTN, where service-based networking approaches (ICN, DTN, etc.) are extremely relevant to achieve a smooth integration.
- Quantum technologies, and in particular, QML, as a relevant field, to consider for the overall deployment of large-scale 6G sensing/localization services.
- The development of a human-centric 6G set of services should be based, from the networking perspective, on the integration of social awareness derived from an interdisciplinary approach requiring joint work between computer science and social sciences.

The visions that have been provided are a product of a continuous debate being developed in CONASENSE in the form of scientific outcomes such as publications, talks, brainstorming events, and projects that bring together international experts worldwide, to discuss the CONASENSE 6G development.

This vision continues to be regularly developed, being the next steps in the debate of sustainability and greenness integration into 6G services, and what technological developments are required, to make this vision a reality.

Index

About the Editors

Prof. Dr. Ramjee Prasad, Fellow IEEE, IET, IETE, and WWRF, is a Professor of Future Technologies for Business Ecosystem Innovation (FT4BI) in the Department of Business Development and Technology Aarhus University, Herning, Denmark. He is the Founder President of the CTIF Global Capsule (CGC). He is also the Founder Chairman of the Global ICT Standardization Forum for India, established in 2009. He has been honored by the University of Rome "Tor Vergata," Italy as a Distinguished Professor of the Department of Clinical Sciences and Translational Medicine on March 15, 2016. He is an Honorary Professor at the University of Cape Town, South Africa, and the University of KwaZulu-Natal, South Africa, and also an Adjunct Professor at Birsa Institute of Technology, Sindri, Jharkhand, India. He has received Pravasi Bhartiya Samman Puraskaar (Emigrant Indian Honor Award by the Indian President) on January 10, 2023 in Indore. He has received the Ridderkorset of Dannebrogordenen (Knight of the Dannebrog) in 2010 from the Danish Queen for the internationalization of top-class telecommunication research and education. He has received several international awards such as the IEEE Communications Society Wireless Communications Technical Committee Recognition Award in 2003 for making a contribution in the field of "Personal, Wireless and Mobile Systems and Networks," Telenor's Research Award in 2005 for impressive merits, both academic and organizational within the field of wireless and personal communication, 2014 IEEE AESS Outstanding Organizational Leadership Award for: "Organizational Leadership in developing and globalizing the CTIF (Center for TeleInFrastruktur) Research Network," and so on. He has been the Project Coordinator of several EC projects, namely, MAGNET, MAGNET Beyond, eWALL. He has published more than 50 books, 1000 plus journal and conference publications, more than 15 patents, over 150 Ph.D. Graduates and a larger number of Masters (over 250). Several of his students are today's worldwide telecommunication leaders themselves.

Prof. Dr. Rute C. Sofia (Ph.D. 2004) is the Industrial IoT Head at fortiss – research institute of the Free State of Bavaria for software-intensive services and systems. She is also an Invited Associate Professor at University Lusófona de Humanidades e Tecnologias, and an Associate Researcher at ISTAR, Instituto Universitário de Lisboa. Rute's research background has been developed on industrial and on academic context. She was a co-founder of the COPELABS research unit, and the COPELABS scientific director (2013–2017), where she was a Senior Researcher (2010–2019). She has co-founded the Portuguese startup Senception Lda (2013–2019), a startup focused on personal communication platforms.

Her current research interests are network architectures and protocols; IoT; Edge computing; in-network computing; network mining. Rute holds over 60 peer-reviewed publications in her fields of expertise and 9 patents. She is an ACM Europe Councilor; an ACM Senior member, an IEEE Senior Member, and the IEEE ComSoc WICE industry deputy liaison. She was an IEEE ComSoc N2Women Awards co-chair (2020–2021). She is a NetWorld ETP Expert Group Member.

Before fortiss, she was an Associate Professor (COPELABS/ULHT, wireless/user-centric networking; sensing; IoT); she co-lead as senior researcher in the "Internet Architectures and Networking" area of UTM, INESC-TEC (07-10), focus on wireless/cellular network architectures and user-centric networking; she was (04-07) a senior research scientist in Siemens AG and Nokia-Siemens Networks GmbH, focusing on aspects such as fixed-mobile convergence; carrier-grade Ethernet; QoS; IPv6 interoperability.

Rute holds a BEng in Informatics Engineering by Universidade de Coimbra (1995); M.Sc. (1999) and Ph.D. (2004) in Informatics by Universidade de Lisboa. During her Ph.D. studies, she was a visiting scholar (2000–2003) at Northwestern University (ICAIR) and at University of Pennsylvania, MNLab.